Widow in the Woods

by
Beulah "Boots" Brenner

To Joan, who also has a
story to Tell. Best Wishes!
Brots

PUBLISH
AMERICA

blishAmerica
Baltimore

First printing

ISBN: 1-4137-1626-1
PUBLISHED BY PUBLISHAMERICA, LLLP
www.publishamerica.com
Baltimore

Printed in the United States of America

Dedicated to
Barb, Rick, David and Joann
who supported me in my Colorado Quest

ACKNOWLEDGMENTS

My dear friend Elizabeth Testa who edited several manuscript drafts and lifted my spirits.

The many colleagues and friends in Illinois who encouraged and worked tirelessly to make the Colorado dream come true.

The many new friends in the Rocky Mountains who came to my aid and comfort and who asked, "Is *Widow in the Woods* finished yet?" to keep me going.

Dr. Joseph Murphy for his sensible remedies to keep me physically fit to write and be the widow in the woods.

My niece Diana Hoehn and her husband Adolph for giving us refuge during the Missionary Ridge Fire.

My nephew Roger Norris who struggled to make me computer literate.

My nieces Emily and Anne, and their husbands Roger and Tony, for keeping an eye on me without intruding on my independence.

TABLE OF CONTENTS

Introduction

"Sell the house? I love that house!" son Rick said in a loud and pained voice. I had just broken the news that on retirement about three years hence I would be moving to Colorado. As a first response, I might have hoped for more enthusiasm, but Rick had spent the better part of his childhood in our comfortable old home.

And so began a journey of anticipation, anxiety, doubts and reaffirmation, a journey to adventure, to a new world and a new beginning.

This book is about the various steps leading up to great changes in my life in 1984, at age 62, a widow of 7 years. The message I would like to leave with you is that your world doesn't need to end when you lose your lifetime partner through death or divorce. It can be a time of new challenges and satisfying joys.

My journey would take me from an Illinois community of 30,000 people, elevation of some 600', to a one-acre "spread" in a Ponderosa pine tree woods in the southwest Colorado Rockies, elevation of 7,800'. One neighbor would live across from my driveway, about 30 feet up and the next closest neighbor would be about 500 feet east at the end of the cul de sac. I would find the nearest community, Bayfield, 7 miles south with then a population of about 600. The larger town of Durango was 28 miles to the west.

I will tell you of my thoughts, anxieties, setbacks and anticipation. No, I was not crazy, as some of my colleagues suspected at the time. I didn't rush off willy-nilly, but considered my finances, figured what I would need to live on and recognized that I would need to scale back my standard of living. That was O.K.; I had never felt I had to have the latest in home or personal fashions so I felt I could manage on less money. I thought. I studied. I investigated. I planned. I was committed to my dream!

My hope is to inspire other adventurers to follow their own calculated-risk dreams, even if more timid people consider these moves to be foolhardy. Women have always met challenges. Don't imagine gender is a bar to the pursuit of a dream. Of course a woman alone can do what I did. Consider what roles a woman fills as "housewife" and working mother. She is a supply sergeant, transportation director, in charge of the mess, oversees maintenance (often taking care of it herself), and is a finance officer, nurse, comforter and scheduler extraordinaire! I was well-equipped for my adventure. Most likely, you are, too.

My tale has something for everyone: Adventure, close calls, wildlife (animal, but a little of mine!), domestic animal companions, house building, romance, political involvement, church and civic responsibilities and meeting advancing age head-on.

Now, what in the world is that widow doing in the woods? She is having the time of her life.

ONE
What Came Before the Woods?

Flashback to 1943. In September of that year, when I was 21, I was hired as the first Girl's and Women's Work Secretary at the Kankakee, Illinois YMCA. One of my duties included securing leaders for the boys' Hi-Y Clubs. The minister at my church recommended a new young reporter in town. I called and left several messages at *The Daily Journal* for Gil Brenner to contact me. One of the girls in our new Tri-Hi-Y Clubs, Elizabeth "Tiz" Folds, was working at the *Journal* for the summer and when Gil asked her about me, she saw her chance to pull a trick on him. She told him I was about 65, skinny, wore glasses and would never let up on him so he'd better go see me.

On that day I was filling in at the front desk. Gil asked for Miss Chatfield. When I confessed my identity, his eyes opened wide and he stared so long I was sure some of the top buttons of my new scoop neckline dress were not fastened. Before he left, he not only agreed to lead the Hi-Y Club, but I sold him a $15 membership! He remained an active member in and spokesman for the Y for life.

That encounter led to our courtship, engagement and marriage on June 1, 1946.

Our daughter, Barbara Jean, was born in 1949 and son, Richard

Joseph, was born in 1953. You will learn more about all of us in the succeeding pages.

Now we will shoot ahead to 1975. Gil was a newspaperman – columnist, editor, feature writer – and an active athlete. He was a local tennis champ in both singles and doubles and spent many hours teaching tennis, especially to young people. As Youth Editor at *The Kankakee Daily Journal*, Kankakee, Illinois, he covered high schools in the surrounding area. Gil and I also had contact with high school kids through our work at the Presbyterian Church for 18 years, with one brief interruption.

In spite of being a little overweight, Gil appeared to be in good health and followed a vigorous schedule. But soon I noticed in him increasing fatigue and a slight weight loss when I knew he wasn't watching his diet that closely. I urged him to see his doctor…no, I *nagged* him! This wasn't the way we usually functioned with each other, but I was sure all was not well. This happened twice, with the doctor missing the diagnosis both times. When Gil returned from the second doctor visit, he threw his keys on the counter with an angry, "There, now are you satisfied? The doctor said to lose a little weight and slow down!"

This attitude was not at all typical of him. In retrospect, I think his anger was concealing his concern that he, too, felt there was something wrong. In due course this proved to be true and he was hospitalized with a bowel obstruction. This was in 1977 and the more sophisticated cancer diagnostic tools were not available then. The colon resection was successful but the cancer had already metastasized to the liver.

These were pre-hospice days and I cared for him at home. Kankakee Federal Savings & Loan, where I was employed, allowed me to complete some of my office work at home, using a courier between the two places. I also had the support of church, family and friends during his chemotherapy. When he could no longer leave the house, the doctor came to him. He continued to write his *Spare Type* column, which consisted of bits of information about people, who were interesting but not substantial enough for an entire story. Kind of like a gossip column, but good stuff. He even started a new one called *Musings of a Writer,* in which he detailed some of his experiences in 31 years of writing, along with continued advice to young people through an amusing device. He pretended that just after his chemo shot, he could understand the communication between our mother cat Tiger, and her sometimes-wayward son, Rascal. She pointed out some of Rascal's errant ways and what troubles his behavior could lead to. It wasn't hard for Gil's admirers to make the connection to their own lives.

He told the readers about his cancer battle at a time when people didn't use the C-word very much. That triggered an avalanche of letters from his followers, telling him of their experiences with the awful disease and what they were doing about it. They *wanted* to be open with people about what they were facing. They also told him other things about their families, providing much information for the *Spare Type* column. I started alphabetizing the letters to be easier to locate when he was ready to write the column. After working on about 1,000 of them, I had to stop the practice because he required more care.

He wouldn't take pain pills until after the columns had been written, first at the typewriter in his office, then in longhand in a stenographic notebook, and the last one dictated into a tape recorder when he could no longer hold a pencil. I took that tape into the office to transcribe for the paper. I shut the door, played the tape and typed for a while, cried, then resumed. The voice on the tape was his and yet it was not, but the unmistakable spirit was there. That last column was printed on December 18, 1977. He died on December 19, at age 55.

Throughout my existence I have felt the presence of God in my daily life – even when I made some wrong choices – maybe especially then because I knew He wanted the best for me. And only by following His guidelines would the best life be available to me. God's influence is so interwoven in my activities that praying is automatic and usually informal.

During Gil's illness, I would tell God how I wanted this to turn out, but had to end prayers with, "Nevertheless, not my will but Thine be done." Then I was able to get a restful night's sleep without the aid of drugs.

About a month prior to Gil's death, our daughter Barbara, Director of the Children's Library in Danville, Illinois, at that time, came home with the approval of the Library Director who also felt that home was where she needed to be. At the same time, our son Richard, who was working on his Doctorate in Medical Entomology at Cornell University in Ithaca, New York, was also granted leave to be with his father.

They came just at the time when I could no longer get my husband out of the bathtub where a Jacuzzi gave him welcome temporary relief from leg pain. Prior to their arrival, I had rigged up a Rube Goldberg system of several of his old belts fastened together and strung around the base of the toilet, up over a divider concealing pipes and into the tub. Gil never lost his sense of humor and we had some laughs over how it must have looked as he grasped the circle of belts while I swung him to the edge of the tub. When he was too weak to help in this process, our children came home. Their strong, young arms took over. It wasn't a coincidence – we all felt we were under God's care and protection in this difficult situation. It was a bittersweet time when we all became closer, laughing and loving each other under the shadow of certain death. We three collaborated on writing an epilogue for the newspaper where he had worked for 33 years, relating to his readers how he faced his battle. The outpouring of love and support from the community at his death also sustained his family.

The next month, Doctor Richard Ray, on the board of the Kankakee Chapter of the American Cancer Society, called to ask if I would be the Crusade Chairman for 1978. He had been one of our "kids" in the Youth Fellowship some years back. I told him, "No, the wounds are still too fresh," but he urged me to think it over and he would call back again. It was a hard decision to make. I didn't really want to do it, but finally reasoned that Gil had brought the community a long way in knowing about cancer...maybe this was one last thing I could do for him…finish the education he had started. While it was difficult to do, on looking back, it was good for me. I could still grieve, along with the community, and maybe be beneficial at the same time.

I proposed to the Cancer Board the idea of the Eighteen-Twenty Five Club, based on 5-cents a day for 365 days ($18.25) for the Cancer Society to be used for benefits and research for a cure. The reasoning was that there were many people who felt they couldn't give a large sum, but they could handle dropping a nickel into a can each day.

The Board approved the concept and a committee was formed to implement the plan. My friends, Marian and Ellis Gravlin, who had a graphic arts studio, designed a label for cans provided by the American Cancer Society, which were distributed to area clubs and organizations. They in turn gave them to their members. Banks agreed to serve as collection points. During the Crusade time, I gave many speeches, sometimes two a day, to service clubs and other organizations that had agreed to push the club idea to their members. Numerous people were involved. Gil was so widely known and loved, old and young grieved with us. The result: The Crusade went way over goal. Families were talking more openly about cancer and checking the seven warning signals.

TWO
A New Volume Opens

I was grateful for my interesting job in the marketing department at Kankakee Federal Savings & Loan Association. As I adjusted to widowhood at age 55, I truly knew the value of full-time employment to ease grief when my mind had to be focused elsewhere for eight hours a day. And that's when friends really count. My fellow members in the Round Table Club saw to it that I didn't drop out by calling to pick me up for the monthly meetings. On another level, this naïve widow didn't learn until later when recounting an episode to a friend what one man *really* meant when he said, "If you need anything, day or *night* (his emphasis), just call me!"

For several years, my job had involved writing and editing a quarterly magazine informing members of our Association's Savers Club about special discounts available to them for showing their club cards, and what group travel opportunities were planned for that quarter. With help from several others in the department, I planned and frequently escorted these trips, which ranged from one-day outings to two-week trips, using buses, planes and cruise ships. They were very popular.

Even the designated sign-up days for the trips had a holiday atmosphere. They were held at 6 a.m. on Saturday when the S & L was normally closed because many of the tellers and other employees were needed to take names, addresses and payments or deposits for the trip(s) of their choice. Because people came so early to get in the line that extended down the street and around the corner, the time-temperature-message sign on our building had to explain that there was no "run on the bank" – it was trip sign-up day! One avid member was usually the first one in line, arriving as early as four in the morning.

Escorting those trips was fascinating. I got to know our customers on a more personal level not possible in their brief visits to the office. Many of the travelers did not know each other so usually once the bus got rolling, the escort put in motion a "mixer" plan. The persons on the aisle seats directly behind the driver were asked to move back one aisle seat, and the person in the last row to move directly across the aisle. The aisle seat holders in that row moved up one seat with the one in the first row moving over behind the driver. The idea was to get to know the new seat partner. Anticipating that not all people are adept at small talk with strangers, the escort suggested some questions – where do you live, do you have children, where do you work, do you have hobbies – to get the conversational ball rolling. Usually the conversation started out quietly but as the passengers discovered friends in common, or similar interests, the noise level rose until it sounded like a very large, busy beehive.

This method resulted in an important "group" feeling early in the trip. Instead of "us" and "them," it quickly became "we," which helped the escort because everyone looked after each other, becoming concerned if someone was late in returning to the bus.

In the meantime, the escort was also chatting with people and picking up information for later use. When it was time for a break or lunch stop, one side was designated to exit first but rather than just alternate each time, the escort introduced a little element of mystery. She might ask, "Where is the woman who has 11 grandchildren?" When the hand went up, it was declared that she needed a little extra attention so she could leave first, with the rest of the people on that side to follow her. Or, "Where is Joe? He's always hungry so we better let him be the first in line for lunch!" The system made good use of the information gathered, and was a way to have a little fun while avoiding a mad dash for the door with resulting gridlock in the aisle. When the scenery was familiar to everyone or was not interesting, games and songs mixed the unmixables, who were not unmixables for very long.

Once in a great while disaster struck. One woman's money was lifted from her purse in a restroom near a big city. She was unaware of it until the thief tossed the purse back over the stall door, hitting her in the head. This resulted in escorts being supplied with extra money in case a loan was needed. Remember, these were our customers!

Occasionally first aid was needed after a tumble. Once a diabetic traveler was having difficulty; however, a nurse on board had some orange juice which saved the day, but thereafter, diabetics were required to have a traveling companion equipped to handle such an emergency.

I responded to a midnight knock on my door for an emergency that was easily handled but it made me aware that my nightgown and robe were only so-so. They were decent enough, but the pieces didn't match. Once back home, I purchased an attractive pajama/robe set. Of course, there were no more midnight callers.

One woman who was caring for her ailing mother had signed up for a seven-day trip to Colorado when the mother took a turn for the worse, not knowing anyone in the family and just generally unaware. The long-term caregiver tearfully told the doctor about the trip and said she would cancel it. "No," he thundered. "You have been giving your mother excellent and constant care and are worn out. You *need* this trip." Knowing the mother wouldn't know whether the daughter was there or not, he added that if she died during the next week, he'd just put mother on ice until she returned. No, mom didn't die that week and the daughter was grateful to the doctor for his compassion.

Crawford Bus Company, the bus company we used, usually assigned one particular driver to many of our trips so he was well known to repeat travelers. In fact, he became so familiar with us, and one passenger in particular, that he and she took their one-week honeymoon on a trip to Florida with 43 of us along!

A wildly popular offering was the Mystery Trip. Most of us like surprises. We like wondering what is inside an attractively wrapped package, and I think that was part of the appeal. Our group travel had been in operation for several years when these trips were offered, so they trusted our planning. I described the Mystery Trips in the magazine through poetry. I didn't reveal the destination, which had not been offered before, or special events – only the dates, length of trip and cost, with a few hints as to appropriate clothing.

It always struck me as incongruous that a Savings & Loan Association, which advocates prudent use of your money, could in effect say, "It will cost you (from $15 or so up to as much as $500), you won't know where you are going, and it will last x number of days," – and members would flock to sign up or get on a waiting list!

When the first Mystery Trip was planned, a day trip, we did it cautiously because we were in uncharted waters, and arranged for only one bus. On sign-up day we filled four buses and still had a waiting list. Luckily, we were able to increase all reservations. That trip was to Chicago and included stops to view Chagall mosaics and sculptures (free), a visit to a new vertical mall (lunch on their own) and a stop at a suburban dinner theater on the way home. The only costs were for the transportation and the dinner theater – a total of $18. Surprisingly, some of the participants had not been to Chicago – only 65 miles away – for 20 years.

All subsequent Mystery Trips enjoyed the same popularity. Even though members liked the surprise element, some of them still tried to find out where we were going by questioning other employees, few of whom knew any details. Maybe these people had a strong need to "be in the know." Only the department head, the trip planner and the head teller, who had to issue checks for advance trip payments, had any knowledge of the destination. One wily member even called the owner of the bus company in another city to pry out information, but he just said he didn't know where we were going, that he'd find out when he came to pick us up. A little thinking about it on the part of the caller would have indicated that he had to know in order to quote us a price. But we were glad he wasn't questioned further. Another caller said her husband had a hernia and wanted to know if a lot of walking was required or should he have the operation right now.

This wonderful, interesting job kept me from dwelling too much on my singleness. While not actively looking for another husband, I was open to the possibility and had some offers I wasn't interested in. Friends said I was too choosy. I guess I was. My husband had always encouraged me to step out and try new things as a stay-at-home mother. He encouraged me to take adult education courses or exercise classes at the Y, or to dust off my violin and play in the Kankakee Symphony Orchestra, or in the pit orchestra for high school musicals. And we both worked closely with young people at the church. I wasn't sure I could find that again. I had seen too many widowed people marry hastily because they didn't want to be alone, with disastrous results. No husband is better than the wrong husband, I reasoned. And, besides, no one had generated "sparks" in me, and that was a must!

Four years later, I picked up a virus at a convention in Florida and was plagued with a throat infection from mid-February to April. I was well enough to go to work but my energy was low, and so was my outlook on life. One evening that spring, which usually gave me a boost after Illinois winters, I contemplated my dreary life: work, come home, unsatisfactory TV dinner before equally unsatisfactory TV shows, read newspaper, go to bed – repeat next day. I did things with friends and felt my life was O.K. if not fantastic, but toward the end of that April I came to the realization that if changes were to occur, I had to make them – there would be no rescuing knight on a white charger.

In late June of 1981, my friend Elinor Kukuck, a retired former colleague, and I took a vacation trip to Forest Lakes, a mountainside development in Colorado. We visited another retired colleague, Dora Koski, who had moved to the southwest Colorado Rocky Mountains with her husband, Carl. We stayed there several days;

exclaiming over the scenery, intimidated by the mountains (call us prairie chickens), enthralled by the wildlife, and sleeping a lot, as is common for newcomers to the high altitude. During that first week in July, I began a new love affair – with Colorado!

The Koskis' mountain chalet home had a loft overlooking the living room and floor-to-ceiling windows flanking a massive stone fireplace. I was sleeping on a sofa bed in the loft and opened my eyes to the view of tall deep green pine trees against a breathtaking blue sky. *Oh,* I thought one morning, *wouldn't it it be wonderful to wake up to that every morning!* I immediately dismissed the idea as impossible. Several more days of tourist activity didn't make the thought go away. During the give-and-take mental discussion with the little voice inside of me (sorry, Tom Selleck/Magnum...I've been listening to my little voice for years!), I was forced to ask myself, "O.K...Why *couldn't* I wake up to that every day?"

That did it. On the return trip to Illinois with Ellie driving and me with a notebook at the ready, I listed reasons why a retirement move to Colorado was or was not desirable. At the end of the discussion, standing alone in the not desirable column was the fact that I would leave good friends behind. Well, I could make new friends and the old ones could come visit. O.K....cross that one off.

My children already lived in other cities, and I really didn't want to move to a city where they lived, or to move in with either of them. I was too independent! And besides, it might cause complications for them. What conscientious mother wants to be a damper to possible promotional moves for her children? Then the question would arise for them – what do we do about Mom? I could imagine the discussions then if I moved to either of their cities, "But Mom just moved here to be near us, how can we pick up and move to South Carolina (or California or wherever) for that new job?" Shudder...I didn't want to do that. We concluded that since I wasn't near them now, I could continue to be with them by telephone from Colorado.

The next item on the list was retirement. I would have to wait three years, until age 62, but could sell the house and prepare for the move during that time. O.K. No problem there. Or at least that's how it seemed at the moment. Then I pondered, *would I buy a house or build?* Probably build because my son-in-law, David, had polio as a child and was in a wheelchair so I would want to make it as accessible as possible. O.K., then look for a lot.

Often on vacation people think *that* location would be a great place to live, but they usually lose interest back home in the usual routine. It didn't happen to me this time – I never lost the vision. In September, Ed Zellner, the Colorado real estate agent on the lookout for a good lot for me, called Dora to report, "Have I got a good deal for Boots!" She urged him to call me and when he did, I was in the middle of preparing the quarterly Savers Club magazine. Not wanting to buy a pig in a poke (am I maligning the pig?), I finished the magazine, and then flew back to Colorado in mid-October to look over the lot.

The view from the top of my property. Photo/Anne Schrier

Colorado is beautiful in every season but that October she was resplendent. Smart realtor. First he showed me just lots surrounded by trees, no view; or very small lots in the meadow with close neighbors. Then he showed me THE lot on the downhill side of

Grassy Mountain in the San Juan Range of the Rockies, at about 7,800 feet elevation, with Ponderosa pine woods, scrub oaks, wonderful views of two mountains, the meadow, the river and those blue, blue skies. I typed the contract for him, put $500 down, with the balance of $7500 to be paid by mail at closing in December of 1981. Then, I was a Colorado property owner!

On that memorable October visit, my hosts Dora and Carl introduced me to residents who would be my neighbors in the Forest Lakes community. I felt an immediate rapport with them and was eager to see them again. How could I stand the waiting?

THREE
Sorting Through Life's Accumulations Treasure and Trash

When I first broached the idea of buying a lot and moving to Colorado both the kids were in favor of it, then things plummeted for Rick, as I mentioned earlier.

After a quick lesson in economics, his initial dismay vanished and he understood that I couldn't build a house until I first sold one, and he then gave his whole-hearted support. Of course he loved the house. It was a wonderful place for a young boy to grow up; cubby holes under the three porches, full basement, full attic, a fireplace, a sleeping porch and a screened porch with no outside entry across the front of the house. He was in third grade when we moved there and so bonded to it more than Barb did, who was in seventh grade and more interested in bonding with people.

Long before selling, I began to clean out the attic in the fall of 1981.

When you dismantle a 10-room house you've lived in for 23 years, you churn up more than dust. There is nothing that reminds you so forcibly of the passage of time and your own mortality like cleaning out the attic – or the basement or the storeroom or wherever it is you put all those things you just can't part with.

Our attic was the resting place for a variety of no longer in use items – and memories.

On opening the small doll suitcase I saw my little girl creating a new outfit for her Barbie doll. And clever it was, too. She had taken one of her dad's old brown rib-knit socks, lopped off the toe a little way back from the end and…lo!…a charming little hat. Cutting the sock above the heel and discarding the foot part, she used the leg length for a curve-clinging ribbed sheath. Barbie looked fetching in her new hat and shapely knit dress. I was so proud of *my* Barb and her creativity. And I was so glad she could make her own doll clothes, something at which I was very inept.

Then I found the little soft cloth bag of marbles, with its drawstring security closing. My son Rick's generation didn't embrace the fine art of playing marbles like Peck's *Bad Boy* or Mark Twain's mavericks but still they had their season with the mibs, the aggies, the glassies and the steelies. Another box revealed jacks and a crumbling rubber ball – the girls usually excelled at that game – some small metal cars with chipped paint as evidence of the miles they zoomed around to the realistic engine sounds that only small boys do so well. There were rusting darts, battered toy soldiers, assorted Tinker Toy parts sharing the space with plastic building blocks, tennis balls that had lost their bounce, the backpack frame, the butterfly net and…well…you know, the treasures that boys collect through the years. Did his interest in the butterfly net and every insect that crawled or flew signify that he would become a research scientist with a doctorate in Medical Entomology?

I recalled that there might have been other indications of the scientific bent. When he was a child, helping me in the kitchen baking cookies, he asked if he could taste the flour. I was taken aback and said that, yes he could but I didn't know why he would want to. I warned him that someday he might be sorry about what he tasted. Many years later I learned that tasting substances is one method scientists use to analyze the classification – is it sweet or sour? That little research scientist is now the Deputy Assistant Administrator in the United States Department of Agriculture, Agricultural Research Service, Office of Technology Transfer, with offices in Beltsville, MD and Washington, D.C.

Another box yielded an assortment of children's books reserved for future grandchildren. At the sight of them I could see Barb and Rick in various spots and positions around the house – legs over a chair arm, or on backs or stomachs – reading. I had told them books were magic carpets that could take them anywhere in the world. Gil and I were always pleased to see them reading.

Our daughter, who left more athletic pursuits to her brother and father, had more likely stockpiled books, tablets, pencils, crayons and board games. Gifts of these items she welcomed with wide-open arms. She and I said we got our exercise turning the pages of a book. Once she learned to read, Barb and I shared our voracious love of reading, discussing books and the stories they contained. Because Gil and I had a large collection of books, she occasionally selected one from our shelves to read. Her father and I didn't exactly censor any of them, but suggested she might wait until she was older to read a more adult book.

While packing up the books, I recalled that Barb had asked about one with a catchy title that had attracted me, too, "Who's Hiding In My Hide-a-Bed?" (a Book-of-the-Month Club selection by Ann Warren Griffen, published in 1958 by Simon and Schuster). Barb was in high school then. I thought about her request for a minute, then told her she could read it if she wanted to. When we discussed it later I asked her what she thought of it. She replied with disdain, "It was dumb!" That was her first book review. Now she writes book reviews monthly for a Danville newspaper, providing a real service to the community. But that book was not the humorous story we both expected. It was concerned with rather detailed accounts of the heroine's amorous encounters in the sofa bed. And now Barb is and has been the Director of the Danville, Illinois Public Library for more than 25 years. The trend was there all along.

All these treasures brought bittersweet memories of days that were glorious…and would not come again. It was emotionally draining to examine those unbidden memories, to ask again the unanswerable questions. Were we good parents? If so, was it accidental, or with purpose? Did we give them the basic foundation and tools to build strong characters to serve them well in their adult lives? God knows we wanted to.

I would find myself turning aside. Better leave this job for another day – work with the more impersonal items in the attic – like the old carpets not good enough for the living room but too good to discard those many years ago, or the battered tables, the folding chairs that didn't fold properly, the oval coffee table of another day. But each of those invoked memories too. The rim of the coffee table once secured a sheet of glass that protected the baby and family pictures beneath it. And I could see small Barbara reaching for the covered candy dish. I could see Rick in the basement laying out the track of his small race set on the old linoleum-covered table that was left behind by previous owners.

Inevitably I would have to procrastinate out of exhaustion. O.K., tomorrow I will sort these things into piles for Barb, for Rick, for me to take to Colorado. Start another pile for the Baby Tenda and other items for the moving sale, yet other piles to give to charity, or to end up in the trash.

Self-coaching became an art: Concentrate on the new life you will lead in Colorado. Life as it was is gone. Barbara and Rick have finished college and are engrossed in their careers and marriages, as they should be. My husband has been nursed through his last sad illness. Two more chapters in my life – child rearing and marriage – have been closed. Look ahead to retirement and a lessening of responsibilities. Look ahead to the healing mountains and cleansing streams. You'll always be there for your children but now you are free to think of your own needs and wants. As poet Robert Browning penned, "…The best of life, for which the first was made, Our times are in his hand."

On August 21, 1981, in celebratory red ink, I started marking off the days to retirement at 62, and that magic date of March 29, 1984 – 952 days. A new home in Colorado in three years.

I did get the necessary job done before Christmas of that year when Barb and her intended David, and Rick and his wife Joann and her son Tony were there to check over their respective piles. They each took what they could fit into their cars and left larger items for later transportation.

I also asked them to go through the house and indicate which of my possessions they might like to have eventually. They were gratifyingly reluctant to do this, but I convinced them it would be a help to me in time. I assured them that time was very distant, if I had anything to say about it. They complied, sort of.

Two years later, as I watched movers take to a van the items Rick had selected at that Christmas, I was revisited with nostalgia as I remembered him growing up, using the backpack frame, the butterfly net, the ping pong table, and especially the small blackboard on which he and his father had kept a running ping pong score during his teen and college years. I remembered the winner's marks on one especially long game: 1 1 1 1 1, with the last mark going almost to the bottom of the blackboard. Years later, Rick still has that board, with score preserved, in the office at his home. Our memories are precious.

The four of us in 1976. Photo/ Ellis Gravlin

FOUR
Keeping an Eye on the Goal

In the meantime, I made another trip to Colorado to talk with contractors and residents about the type of house to build, looked at houses built by prospective contractors and others to get an idea of a house plan I wanted to follow. I was grateful for the advice of my Forest Lakes friends.

Word of warning to would-be house builders wherever you may be: Ask to visit houses built by specific builders and query the owners as to construction mistakes that had to be corrected or re-done, either by the contractor during the warranty period or later by the sad home owner. Sometimes the errors can be very minor and not held against the construction crews. But some people I have known had major problems because the contracted plumber was irresponsible and didn't supervise his inexperienced workers. Others used a builder whose work they had not checked out and spent a lot of money replacing tile, the roof and various other elements, caused primarily because he cut too many corners. This precaution can save you money, time and frustration. And regarding competent builders, the man who built that Kankakee house deserves a medal. He was a contractor, building it for himself: Solid oak flooring and woodwork, for one thing. Years later when we put in self-storing aluminum storm windows and screens, the installer was impressed because he had to make a frame adjustment on only one window – and there were 52 of them, from about 2 feet square (in closets) to full-sized ones. Craftsmanship and pride…not always in evidence today.

Back in Illinois, I confronted the biggie – trying to sell our beautiful old house, built in 1913. It took a long time for me to stop referring to things as "our" when by this time I was the only one left in the nest – and now after 25 years, I still lapse into it in unguarded moments, like this one. When questioned on that pronoun by people who know I am a widow, I tell them that my cats are part owners with me.

Alas, it was a depressed market in my town in 1982, '83 and '84 when I was trying to be a seller and was I depressed by that! Several national companies had left the area, taking some employees with them. Their homes were on the market as well as the homes of others who had secured employment in different localities, so the town was glutted with houses for sale.

I kept a diary during this period which tells of the despair, longing, hopelessness and then renewed enthusiasm – the whole bit. Here are a few excerpts, bad sentence construction and all.

It is 12:25 a.m. on Tuesday, Aug. 30, 1983. I awoke about an hour and a half ago…thinking about my future in Colorado and impatient to get on with it. Maybe my wakefulness is partly the result of the delicious but too-much pizza I had after golf with my teammates from the office. But it is not an uncomfortable wakefulness.

***

I'm frustrated. My house is not sold, after being on the market for 2 summers. I thought surely someone would be eager for it. It truly is a wonderful family home – maybe not enough bathrooms to please most people, but it has been adequate for the 10 years four of us were here.

31

Following God's plan for me is something I truly want to do, but how can I be sure of what it is? I feel I was led to Colorado when Ellie and I visited Dora and Carl in 1981 because I was ready to be impressed by it.

I feel it was God's leading that made a beautiful lot available to me at a price I could afford – $8,000. And Ed Z's influence that got the initial excavation done, still with no bill to me. How can I make it up to him for strengthening my dream?

The first house plan I looked at is the one that keeps coming back to me – and that I can visualize myself in – although I need to reverse my thinking and visualizing because I reversed the plans to accommodate an added garage, attached, so David could have access to the main living level, as well as the lower level (to be used when company comes to visit – in quantities!). The entire house will be wheelchair accessible. Someday that may be necessary for me if my arthritis continues to develop. But I won't worry about that.

I'm trying to be ready for my new life – bought the 4-wheel drive car needed in the mountains.

I have now measured my furniture and will reduce paper replicas to scale to see what will fit in the house – and what I should discard. Probably I should do more weeding out of things I will not be taking but I hesitate to tear up the place too much in case someone wants to see the house. These are rough times in the housing market – maybe I should come down some more on the price. I really don't want to be greedy, but I want enough to build my "dream house" in Colorado, and it really is a modest one compared to many of them.

Between my pension and social security I won't be rolling in money but it should be adequate because I'm really not an extravagant person. I don't feel as if I have to have everything I see or "the latest" in anything. In fact, sometimes "the latest" has become "old hat" before I discover its existence! [Author's note: I am still driving that American Motors Eagle – 20 years later.] *If I can make a little now and then on free lance writing – and maybe do something about group travel, that should keep me interested in life.*

Seven more months and two days to retirement! I am as eager for it as I was for my first job – and much more secure about it. I don't feel 61+ most of the time. Now and then I think, "You must be crazy – going to live on that mountain at your age!" But I really and truly want it – I can almost taste it! In my mind's eye I can look out on the mountains from my deck or the windows and almost see the deer and elk gently walking among the trees on my lot – or across the road. Oh, please, God, let it be your dream for me too!

As I wrote that last line, my body was wracked by sobs – so afraid am I that this deepest wish may not be granted to me. When I think it might not come true, it is so hard to pray, "Thy will be done." I don't want to give up on this dream – I don't!

It's too hard to write while you are crying!

It didn't last long – but I do have those moments of doubt more often than I like. My faith must not be strong enough – and yet I really feel that God has led me thus far, why do I doubt that the rest will come? I am too impatient. Maybe there is something else I need to learn before the house is sold. What is it?

My good Catholic friends, Rita and Bernadette, have brought me the statue of St. Joseph. I have buried him in the back yard, according to their instructions. Is that blasphemous for me – a Protestant to do that? They offered it out of friendship and I accepted it in the same spirit, and have faith that God listens to all of us, whatever our religious persuasions. And I want this so much I'll accept

help from any quarter. They are praying for my dream, too.
It's now 1:20 a.m. and I have much work to do at the office tomorrow – magazine deadline again. I need to sleep but I am so worked up, I'm afraid it will be long in coming. I'll try reading again for a while.

***

A month later – and a wonderful thing has happened to me! Shortly after I wrote the above at the end of August, I began to be a little uncomfortable about my daily prayers to "Sell the house! Sell the house!" I began to pray that I would be strengthened in my faith that God is in charge and will orchestrate things in His own "time" – and that if my Colorado dream is not to be or is to be delayed a little, I will be strong enough to accept whatever I must do instead. It's like a burden has been lifted from my shoulders! I am just not up tight about it anymore. I still want it very much but I seem more content to "let it happen" and not force it. My prayers also include a young family needing a good house like this. In the meantime, I have been cleaning out bookcases, drawers and the kitchen desk and storage cabinet. I am getting ready – for whatever.

Those cleaning out times are really trips down memory lane – very bittersweet. Old letters bring back college days of Barb and Rick like it was yesterday. I found a small notebook in which D.O.D. [Author's note: Dear Old Dad, our affectionate name for him taken from an ancient Proctor's Toaster Commercial] *had recorded his garden yields for several years – and for a few minutes, I was out with him at Eva Park's garden, working with the warm sun on our backs.*

One day I came across the guest book from his funeral – along with his lists of people to write thank you notes to for flowers or gifts while he was hospitalized. The list was long, but he insisted on writing the notes himself – as he should. There was an even longer list he never saw – the notes that I wrote to people who sent memorials and flowers. It took me several weeks but still it was comforting to know he had so many friends.

I can only do those clean-out jobs for 2 or 3 hours at a time – too emotional. Then I try to do something physical for a while. Twice I went out and played golf. At other times I mowed the lawn, or cleaned the house or did laundry. I think the hardest "clean out" places are behind me now. I saved some of the letters and cards to use as story ideas and background.

Barb is a wonderful letter writer – so creative – and draws word pictures in every line. Not so with Rick. His letters were (and are) very much to the point. "Got your check. Thanks a lot. Will do so and so with it, or will be home Sat. at 6 p.m. See you." But on the rare occasions when he wrote a long one – the scientist shows through. Steps A, B and C with these results.

Rascal-cat lies on the bed at my feet – partially on them – watching as I write, then nodding off now and then, risking a peek with one eye.

The realtor wanted to show the house to a young man yesterday (Wed. 9/28). She called me at the office to say she couldn't get the door open! I told her how to pull the handle toward her as she turned the key and she left to try it again. She called later and said she still couldn't get it, and that Arlean came over from next door but she couldn't make it work either. We arranged her appointment for 5:15, right after work. When I got home I came in the back way and went through to open the door but the knob wouldn't turn! What a way to impress someone with your house! I took them through the back door (he looked so young!) and left them to go work on the front door. After a few unsuccessful tries, I finally got it to turn and open. I will have to get that fixed. Think the problem is in the knob shaft. Never happened before that I am aware of.

I had also made an appointment for about the same time for a furnace inspection. I want to be able to tell the new owners that the furnace is in fine shape – and now I can. He only had to replace the belt on the blower motor. Said it is a very quiet running furnace and should give at least 10 more years of service. They made them to last in those days!

The young man's wife is coming to town on Friday (tomorrow) and I heard him and Betty discussing which ones they will bring her to look at – and this house is one of them!

Yes, I am excited but I am also calm about it and ready to accept the fact that they may not want it. And maybe the time isn't right for me. Lloyd said theirs sold right at the time they needed the money from it to pay on the one they are building near Marion, IL.

Lord, I believe – help my unbelief.

This was a real roller-coaster time for me, wanting so much to be in Colorado and knowing that part of my life couldn't begin until the house was sold. I continued to play golf, clean out drawers and cabinets and do tasks that God couldn't do for me: repeatedly telling myself that God had brought me this far and surely He would bring me the rest of the way. Then came retirement and my daily schedule changed.

FIVE
Finally – The Retirement Party!

The big day came on my birthday – March 29, 1984. It started in the morning before the Association opened for business with presentation of gifts from the Gift Committee (a food processor, for my retirement cooking and eating!), and special gifts from my department relating to my admiration of Tom Selleck.

Given my age at the time (62) and Tom Selleck's (around 40), maybe I need to clarify that admiration. When his Magnum series was in full swing, son Rick was in college and there was some resemblance between them – each had curly hair and a mustache and are truly nice guys. What really cemented my admiration was the way Rick greeted our cats when he came home and the way Tom Selleck greeted the vicious dogs at the estate: "Hi Ya, Guys!" When I explained this to my colleagues, I got the sarcastic rejoinder, "Yeah, Boots, he reminds you of your son!"

If you weren't a Tom Selleck/Magnum fan when his series was popular you may not understand what I meant when I wrote of "my little voice" speaking to me. Magnum had a little voice that pointed him in the right directions in solving his detective cases. Long before Magnum, I was listening to my little voice.

That explains their special gifts to me: A Tom Selleck mug

emblazoned with the excuse "I'm saving myself for Tom Selleck," a Tom Selleck button, and a near-life-size color poster, later laminated to make it drool proof by my friends at the graphic arts studio, which printed our Savers Club magazine. You will hear more about that poster later. After retirement, I received a letter from Jim Schneider, President of the Association, along with a cartoon strip, *Mother Goose & Grimm*, by MPeters. It depicted two of the characters seated back to back, with one of them facing a TV and clutching a Cubs pennant. He says, "I sure hope we win the game today...Maw, did you ever want somethin' so bad that it hurt?" She replies, "Tom Selleck." That was the year the Cubs almost won, and verifies that "The Boss" didn't understand the attraction either.

At least two years prior to my retirement I had related to a number of my colleagues a strange dream in which I seemed to be out at our junior college and lost in a maze of corridors. I went in to an optician's office to ask directions. Why it was at the college, I don't know, but then, dreams don't have to make sense! He finished with a patient, and then introduced himself as John Doe (fictitious name used here to protect the innocent). He was a tall, handsome man in the early forties, clothed in a professional white lab coat, and asked how he could help me. I told him I was lost and then he put his arm around me and kissed me, much to my surprise, but I rallied and said, "How nice!" [Remember, I had been a widow for 5 years!]

When I awoke, the name was so vivid and clear that I went to the phone book to see if there was such a person in the area. There was! Colleague Dianne Loica said we had a customer by that name but in no way did he meet my description of the romantic man. We laughed about it – and then promptly forgot about it.

Late in the afternoon on Retirement Day, a farewell reception was held for me in the company lunchroom. I was chatting with the attendees when Dianne came to me and said there was someone there who wanted to meet me. This good-looking fellow came over to me, shook my hand and said, "My name is John Doe," and he kissed me! I turned beet red and stammered around until Dianne took pity on me and confessed.

The handsome man was the husband of our new Personnel Director. I had to admit the "gotcha" was a good practical joke – and a tribute to Dianne's memory.

I really was retired!

SIX
Learning How to be Retired

.

You might not think I would have to *learn* how to be retired but
my work ethic was persistent. Reading in the middle of the day or
before all the chores were completed brought a dose of guilt, and still
does years later. Now back to the diary and the waiting.

*April 2, 1984. This begins the tale of my retirement! It
is a Monday – the first when I did not have to go to work.
(I didn't go Friday, the 30th, but that didn't really count
because they told me I didn't have to come.) I slept until 7
or a little after, no thanks to Rascal, who tried at 4, 5 and
6 to nudge me from the bed. I exercised on the trampoline
and did the yoga stretching routine for about 20 minutes.
Then a light but leisurely breakfast while I read some more
of "The Blue Highways", a birthday/retirement gift from
Barb & David as I start out on my own blue highways.
After a telephone chat with Ellie, I started the washing,
and then went to clean up the weekend clutter and put
away the double-celebration gifts. Thank you notes are
next on my agenda. This first real day I am playing it by
ear. I'm too new to all this endless time to do what I*

squeezed in before.

My plan, however, is not to let the necessary daily activities steal time from what I really want to do – writing, reading and walking, etc., when I get to the mountains. Now, I hope to sort further the memorabilia of my life during the past 40 years in Kankakee. Oh, how I long for the day when this house is sold! Please, Lord, let it be soon.

April 30th. Yes, I'm still here. It's been a long time since I wrote in this book and I have been down in the valley and up on the mountains on my emotional roller coaster since then. I figured it out last night – the house has been with a realtor 18 of the past 24 months. My contract with one realtor was up Nov. 14, 1983 and in January I gave the listing to Betty, of another agency. She and some other realtors have brought a few people here, but so far, nothing. There is a young couple interested but doubt that they have the money.

The couple that saw the house when the door wouldn't open bought a house in the next block and I am truly glad they did because that widow needed a buyer more than I do. Her husband had died suddenly just a few days before that and had their other house up for sale, too. They planned to live in whichever one didn't sell. A sad case. I must believe that my time is coming soon to sell the house.

I still feel it is in God's hands but I lament my impatience and occasional lapses of faith. Luckily, they don't last long.

The past 7 months really went fast – and now I am retired! The party was fun on my last day and the gift fund presentation with its nonsense about Tom Selleck, and the party with the North End Gang. Jim wrote such nice things about me in Homes and Loans and in the magazine. I am surprised, though, at how seldom I think of the office. I am probably not using my time as wisely as I should, but I'll get the hang of it soon. (Will miss the bigger paychecks!)

I spruced up the yard, which on this very windy day is now littered with fallen tree limbs – some of them of pretty good size – and hope to mow the lawn this week, as well as get in some golf.

Gave Betty a lead on a new engineer coming from Columbus, Ohio, and she told me of another prospect who has sold 2 of his 3 properties in Minnesota and plans to buy in Kankakee. He works at the nuclear plant at Braidwood. Sounds good. (Lord, keep me calm!)

I guess I can see some good in still being here because I have changed my mind about my furniture. When I checked with the movers, I found it would cost about $4,000 to move the things I planned to keep. Some would cost more to move than they were worth! Then I would have to store it out there until the house was built and then move it again – upwards of another $2,000.

When I checked with the auction people, they said their fee is 35% of the proceeds (includes moving it to their warehouse) and he judged it would bring in about $1400. Phooey!

My friends, led by Flonnie, said they would help me hold my own sale and I'd not need to pay a fee. So that's what I plan to do when the time comes. Several have already mentioned they are interested in some of it – Phyllis had her eye on the dining room, Grace liked the twin beds, Marge wanted some chests, Evelyn checked on a bed set for her kids. Maybe it will all work out.

Barb and David were here the weekend I retired and looked over some of the furniture. Have made notes for them and for Rick and family, too. Barb and I hauled out the 2 white metal shelving units that were in the attic. She's using them in their basement. When I went there for Easter (rain, rain, rain!) I took the gray metal filing cabinet for them. Bit by bit. I will give the piano to Rick. They are pleased about that. Barb has her grandmother's piano.

We talked to Rick (in Texas) Easter weekend. He says it is bad in Mexico and they are eager to leave. Country is ripe for revolution. The good news is that he has the job at the USDA lab in Gainesville, Florida and will leave Mexico the 3rd or 4th week in July, or before if it becomes necessary. He has done very well professionally – with new method to control screwworm. Washington Entomology Magazine stopped presses on July issue to wait for his story. Said his phone is tapped (American Embassy listing) and to be careful what I say when I call him. If I get on dangerous ground, he'll tell me he doesn't know what I am talking about – and I should change the subject. Will be careful.

The Glory of the Risen Lord – and still the world has too much darkness and fighting! When will we learn? Do you grow weary with us, Lord?

During my first week of retirement I drew scale (sort of) plans of the house I would like and sent them to Greg Morrison in Colorado. Since then I have thought I should cut down the size, and David suggests a ramp for him to get in the house instead of stair glide or extra garage. Will discuss it with Greg when I see him or call again.

It will be fun picking out new furniture to fit a new house. There is lots of excitement ahead for me! Oh, I want to get on with it!

Ray F. came last Thurs. (4/26) to pick up the wicker couch and chair from the porch. Locked ourselves out in the process and while I located Zona to let me in (she was chatting with the Parkers in their yard), Ray dug up some peonies and lily of the valley plants to take to Southern IL. The porch furniture was in the house when we moved in (1961) – 23 years of good use for us, and how many more for the Ferris family? Was the end of an era to see it go. I remember sleeping on it on hot summer nights before we got the air conditioner – Gil slept inside on the couch – and lying on it to read the Sunday papers. And I remembered sitting on it and crying when a stray cat that Barb let in, killed Sunny, our parakeet. Poor girl – she had no idea he would catch the bird who had freedom from her cage. That porch will be sadly missed – but my new deck overlooking the Pine River Valley and the mountains will more than make up for it.

Oh, yes – I had another tooth crowned – and Dr. Peterson gave me a free cleaning as a retirement gift! I took another important step – went to Beltone for a hearing test and paid a deposit of $350 for a hearing aid. I'm o.k. in most situations but have trouble in meetings catching everything – and have the TV too loud. Maybe my chair is too far from it. Moving it closer might help.

Received a "Retirement Adjustment Allowance" from Financial Institutions Retirement System of $939. Will more than pay for the hearing aid ($700). Also got 1ˢᵗ retirement check from same - $313. Should get SS this week with payment back to January, because I hadn't applied as of age 60 as a widow, which I could have done. Soon will have to watch my pennies! Good incentive to write. That's all now – going to read "Blue Highways" for a while – then Ellie and I will go eat at Chicago Dough (Pizza).

P.S. Received 1ˢᵗ SS check - $600 – on May 3 – then on May 7 received adjustment check dating back to Jan. – $1,279 or something close to it – don't have the record right here. No, that's wrong, the larger check was my income tax refund. The adjustment will come after I file my 1984 income tax return.

***

May 9, 1984 – I never intended to keep a daily diary, so there!

In the month since I last wrote in this book (I have another one going, too!) I have sorted out a few of the many books I must go through. Trouble is – I find too many that I want to read and that slows up the job.

I just made an executive decision! I'm going to just use this book from now on.

As I wrote on the other sheets – I was examined for a hearing aid. It came Monday and I went to get it (May 7). I'm having problems with it – and except for meetings, etc., I don't think I really need it. Have to go for an adjustment next week, so will keep trying it out. If I go to Barb's for Mother's Day or if they come here, I'll try it while they are around watching TV and talking softly, as they do. It seems at times as if it doesn't really fit in my ear right – sometimes, not every time, when I bend over or move my head, it seems to burst out loud with sound – too much, then. is nerve-wracking, but I'll give it a fair trial. He said I have 30 days to try it. If it doesn't work out right, I'll get a refund. Time to sort books again. See you later.
***

Thought of one more thing. Maybe now things will start moving on the house! Someone locally (can't remember who) said I shouldn't have put the St. Joseph statue in a glass jar – just bury it in the dirt. Then I hear on Wally Phillip's show that that's right – just bury the statue and after the house sells, dig it up, wash it off and display it. So that's what's wrong!

I dug it up and to my surprise there was water in the jar. If St. Joseph has the power to intercede, I would think he could do it through glass – and maybe water too, but now we'll see what happens. (Even to a Presbyterian.)

***

Sun. June 3, 1984. The urge to write seems to be on a monthly basis! Two months into retirement and I am still here – with my unsold house. I cannot believe it is taking so long

I went down to Southern Illinois last week, carrying out some of the plans I made last year to visit friends and relatives before I go "west". Visited Ray and Lloyd Elizabeth in their stunning new house near Goreville. Ray designed it and can be very proud of it – and Lloyd's decorating is superb. Lloyd says I should offer a bonus of $1,000 to the real estate salesman who sells mine. Maybe I will – I am so anxious to get on with my plans.

I received an answer to my letter to the Morrison Brothers, builders in Colorado, along with a bid. It's high but it includes some things I have since planned to eliminate anyway – like the stair glide. I plan, if the house doesn't sell before then, to fly out there Tues. June 12 to stay w/Dora & Carl and talk to the Morrisons – get answers to a lot of things – then come back the 19th.

Betty has brought another couple that like the house but aren't sure they want to buy or rent because he only expects to be at the Braidwood Nuclear plant for 3 years. Another one wants the house but I don't think they can come up with the money. Another realtor is checking out an auction possibility. Lots to think about.

Choosing books to "go west" was more difficult than I expected. It was like abandoning old friends. Some of the books had been on our shelves a long time.

It is hard selecting the books to take with me! Have packed 9 boxes to date (with time out for reading). Have to get back to that job this week. Meanwhile, I mowed the lawn, planted flowers (Impatiens by the big tree in front) and seeds – and wait – and wait – and wait!

Oh, yes. While I was in Southern Illinois, Betty's husband came over and buried a St. Joseph statue in the yard – didn't know I had done that. The head of the agency said it was working for other houses and we should do it. Surely we ought to get the job done now!

That hearing aid just did not work for me. Tomorrow I go to try out another kind – totally in the ear – like Pres. Reagan. I'm not convinced I need one – yet.

When things started happening, they happened fast! – and put an end to diary writing for a while. The next entry fills in the details.

Wed. August 29, 1984. Can you believe it?! Here I am in Colorado, living in an 18-foot trailer on my lot at 1180 Deer Ridge Drive. I made the trip to visit Dora and Carl on June 12. When I arrived that night Dora said Betty had called and not to get excited until I heard the reason for the call. It was a toilet overflow in the downstairs bathroom, seeping into the basement! I had left the house about 6:30 a.m. that day. Knowing I would be gone, Betty brought a couple (and their 3 children) to see the house. When she opened the door, she heard the water running. They couldn't budge the shut-off valve so the fellow ran to the basement and grabbed a wrench to do the job. When I talked to Betty that night, I said, sarcastically, that I'll bet he was really impressed with the house, and she said that, yes, he really was. I still didn't get my hopes up when she said it was between my house and one about 10 years old. I had been disappointed too many times before.

The next day at Forest Lakes we went about our planned schedule, which included looking at some houses similar to the one I want to build. We didn't get home until about 11 p.m. The next morning at 7 a.m. Dora knocked on my door and said that Betty was on the line. I said, "Do you suppose ...?" And then followed with, "Nah – probably just more plumbing problems." Betty asked if I wanted the good news first or the bad news. I chose the good – it was *an offer for the house for $70,000 (listed at $74,900) – from the man with the wrench! They wanted the closing no later than July 7th, and first refusal of any furniture I planned to sell. I agreed to everything and was ready for the bad news, which was that the toilet tank had cracked – so water was pouring in from the in-take pipe and pouring right on out the bottom! She had already called a plumber – by chance my own –so it was fixed with no damage to the basement, just a few loosened tiles in the bathroom. The new owner is an executive at Armstrong Cork, so he can replace the tiles easily.*

[Author's note: That house has since sold several times and once was listed for $159,000!]

I stayed in Colorado until the 19th (Super Saver Fare – no refund), talking more positively with the builders! Lots of work ahead of me.

SEVEN
The Moving Sale

I wouldn't have believed I could dismantle a 10-room house, hold a sale, pack what was left to store or take between June 21 and July 5 – but that's what happened, and I could *never* have done it alone. Twenty or more of my friends rallied around to help. I couldn't have *hired* anyone to work as hard as they did! We had long days, sometimes until 11:30 at night. Friend Marian told me that one night she awoke and was so stiff, she had to crawl to the bathroom to get a Tylenol for the pain. I knew just what she meant. For days, every muscle in my body had cried out in protest when the morning alarm went off. Most of the helpers worked daytime jobs, then came to help pack, prepare for the sale or clean the house for the new owners. Here is a salute to you Elinor, Mildred, Bill, Marian, Ellis, Phyllis, Jim, Scott, Virginia, Rita, Bernadette, Flonnie, Keith, Jan, Ruby, George, Evelyn, Frances, Pat, Ralph, Marie, Barb, Bill, Zona and Arlean. Other friends had planned to help but vacations, guests, illness and prior commitments interfered. I'll thank you too for your willingness. I felt your support.

We price-tagged items to be sold and had a preferred customer sale on Wednesday, June 27. This was not advertised and included the people who had been helping me, neighbors, former co-workers at Kankakee Federal and some of the Kankakee Journal staff who had worked with Gil. The public sale was held Saturday and Sunday, June 30 and July 1, from 9 to 4.

I wouldn't have missed that experience for anything. By 9 a.m. a line had gathered out to the street. We had potential buyers enter the kitchen door and exit the front door...past the cashiers! On Saturday, we also had a cashier at the basement door.

There were two workers in each room to keep an eye on things. When I first mentioned having a sale, some friends advised against having it inside the house, warning that people would wreck it. But there was no way I could drag all that stuff outside, where there would be little control over the situation. The people were great. They could tell the house had been well taken care of and treated it with respect. One woman apologized profusely in the basement when her companions scratched off a little paint in a doorway, trying to get the washing machine out. That was the only damage anywhere – and that was inconsequential.

The place was wall-to-wall people and by 10:30 a.m. much of the furniture, household items and tools had been sold. By the end of Sunday, the only things left (other than junk – yes, there was some of that) were a sectional couch in the basement and a dinette set. Friends were planning a garage sale soon so they took the dinette set to sell for me. I left the couch, appreciated by the new owners.

In addition to being hectic, the sale had its light moments too. Kankakee Federal had given employees hams at Christmas so I froze mine, intending to use it for a special occasion. This was it. I baked it and had the rest of the fixin's available for workers to make sandwiches for themselves. The ham was very good – so good that two customers at the sale helped themselves to sandwiches, chips and lemonade. By the time the workers who were making sandwiches for themselves realized that these two were not workers, it was too late. As the satisfied customers left, they said, "This is the best sale we ever went to!"

On Saturday, through an extraordinarily intricate pattern of timing, two of our "salesmen" sold the freezer at almost the same time. The shopper who lost out was very angry and would not believe it was an honest error. The other prospective buyer had asked his salesman to hold it while he ran home to measure the space to be sure it would fit. That message didn't get to the other busy salesman, so he sold it, too. When the measurer returned to buy the freezer, everything hit the fan! The one who lost out went away convinced that Beulah Brenner was a crook. So – who should come on Monday to do the termite inspection but that same person! While I followed him on his inspection round, I was thinking that if he gave a negative report, I would demand a second inspection since he could be biased. Playing for time, I said he looked familiar to me and he replied, dryly, that he was the other one who wanted to buy the freezer. But he was one of those wonderful people at the sale who didn't let his personal feelings interfere, and gave a good report, necessary to complete the sale.

The closing went well and I spent part of the day returning telephones (we didn't own them at that time), changing my address at the post office and tying up loose ends. My realtor did something very nice that other realtors might consider. At the country club, she hosted a "Hello and Goodbye" luncheon for the new lady of the house and for me, inviting various neighbor women.

On the evening of the 10th, I hosted a pizza party at the Chicago Dough Company (that's really the name of the place) to say "thanks and goodbye" to all of those who helped me. All but five invited came. There were 20 of us at tables stretched down the middle of the room. Other customers were served at booths on either side…and I really missed my chance. I didn't look at the bill placed in front of me by the waitress because I was talking, as usual, to some of the group. Soon she hurried back and replaced it with another one. She had given my bill to a stunned young man who expected to pay for two people…not a bill for $94.32.

The great adventure was about to start.

EIGHT
Westward Ho!

Way back months before when no one knew on what date all this would come to pass, my friend Elinor Kukuck had planned to drive out with me. This timing however was not right for her. Not wanting me to drive alone (I was willing but I'm glad I didn't have to), she and Marian Gravlin discussed it. Marian said since she needed a vacation she would accompany Rascal and me, and help with the driving.

That night at the Gravlins, Marian and I planned to wash the clothes we were wearing and shower that night, for an early morning departure. She said she would start the wash while I showered first, and showed me how to operate their tricky, folding shower door. I stripped and handed her my clothes, but I was not an apt pupil with the shower door. I had to yell to her for help since I was trapped in the shower and couldn't get out. After she rescued me, I had to yell to her again to bring me my nightgown and robe that I had neglected to take into the bathroom. Her husband Ellis, trying to watch television in the living room throughout the entire hubbub, probably thought we were in for a great trip if THIS sort of thing continued.

During all the preparation from June 21st on, big old Rascal cat (11years old) did not enjoy the disruption of his routine, nor the people coming and going. He stayed under the porch most of the time, not coming in to eat or drink until things quieted down for the night.

After the closing, he still didn't understand that we didn't live there anymore and continued to stay under the porch while I was at the neighbors. We had food and water out for him, and the new owners put some out for him while I was in Danville. I had an appointment for him with the veterinarian on Monday morning and had to crawl under the porch to drag him out – shouldn't have worn white slacks. I asked the vet if I could board Rascal there until 7:30 a.m. on Wednesday on our way out of town. He agreed, and would tranquilize Rascal before I picked him up. The poor cat was a little spaced out when we got there, but he really was "cool" as the day wore on. I wished they had warned me his eyelids would do strange things reacting to the drugs. I didn't know they have a second eyelid. We were very relieved the next day when he began to come out of it as we started on our journey.

It was with mixed emotions that I left Kankakee that morning. I had been there for 41 years...married there, had two children and buried my husband there, and was leaving behind many friends. I was feeling that tug, but I was also looking ahead with much enthusiasm to starting a new life. Now I would have the fun – and the headaches, people tell me – of building a new house and furnishing it. I could look forward to having those dear old friends come to visit me.

Rascal was a great traveler, thanks to the tranquilizer. For over a year I had taken him for rides in the car to get him used to the cage for a trip longer than the only ones he knew – to the vet's office. I finally opted to take less traveled country roads, with all windows closed so chance passers-by wouldn't hear the horrible howls. I WAS NOT abusing him but it certainly sounded like it.

He seemed content to lie there in the big wire cage, surrounded by boxes, and eating and drinking at night in the motel. He spent part of the first night jumping between my bed and Marian's. The second night was not good for any of us. Luckily, we had two good hours of sleep before Rascal's temporary plumbing problem kept him and us awake. He'd scratch in the litter pan, but couldn't urinate, even though he had been drinking water. Eventually, he succeeded. We finally all settled down about 4 a.m., with the alarm set for 5:15 for an early start. Marian had not realized her alarm clock needed to be wound daily. When she awoke and checked her watch, it was 6:20. We were still O.K. though, because we had forgotten about the time change and gained an hour.

We got to the Koski house in Forest Lakes at 4:30 p.m. on Friday, just in time to unload before a nice rain. We had traveled 1,412 miles and bought 55.2 gallons of gas. The Koskis had gone to Eugene, Oregon, to visit their daughter and I was to house sit until August 5.

We made up for our sleep-deprived Thursday night. With Rascal in the garage, we slept for nine hours. He scared the wits out of us on Saturday when he was missing from about 9:30 a.m. until 6:30 p.m. We just knew he couldn't have sneaked outside because we were so careful going in or out. When a search of the house (twice) didn't reveal him, we began to think that way. When I decided to look up in the loft once more, I heard a cry in response to my call. He had been sleeping the entire day way back in the guest closet under the eaves! We had each searched that place twice, shutting the door because we were so sure he wasn't in there. On Sunday he was missing again but this time we KNEW he was not outside. Late in the day he came strolling out from under Carl's bed...after another long nap.

Marian and I went to check out the trailer the contractor said I might use to live in on the lot while they were building. We decided it would be fine although its 18 feet would have fit in one small part of the basement in Kankakee. All the dead flies in it would present a cleaning challenge.

I took Marian to the airport for her 7 a.m. flight on Monday. It was hard to see her go. We had been through so much together when the house finally sold, and I was deeply grateful for her presence and help on the long journey to my new life.

The first step after Marian left was to firm up a contract with Morrison Brothers, Contractors, and make financial arrangements for construction with the Pine River Valley Bank. It might have been wiser to invest the Kankakee house proceeds at the best interest rate I could find and take out a mortgage on the house. I was so leery of having another mortgage at my age that I opted to deposit the proceeds in a construction account at the bank, at a reasonably good interest rate, and use that to build my new mountain home. I *hated* owing anyone money.

I paid the Morrisons a certain amount for materials at the start, and at intervals as needed to cover allowances for appliances, carpeting, cabinets, etc. I was able to choose those items, staying within the allotted amounts, or paying extra if my selections exceeded the totals. I told you I wasn't "trendy," so I had no trouble keeping the costs down.

One memorable time when I needed to go to the bank to make a transfer, I found myself for the first time in the middle of hundreds and hundreds of sheep being brought home by way of the highway from the high country where they had feasted all summer. In Colorado, livestock have the right-of-way at those times on all roads, even the highway. Those sheep were crowding in front of my car and I kept braking because I was just sure I would hit and kill one! The man in the pick-up truck behind me recognized I was a greenhorn and once, finally, when I was stopped entirely, he left his truck to rap on my window and tell me the proper procedure.

"Don't stop," he said, "just keep going slowly, honk the horn now and then or slap your hand on the side of the car door. They'll move."

He was right. I got over my fear of instant death to the sheep and kept plugging along with the additional tension of worrying if the bank would still be open when I got there. It was. I lucked out.

Since then I have been engulfed in many sheep and cattle drives and only once had to call and reschedule a missed appointment. Later a friend gave me another hint for making them move: Place inside an empty soda can several small pebbles, tape over the opening and shake it out the window periodically.

No matter how many times we find ourselves in the middle of such a movement, there is always plenty to watch. In both spring and fall, there are ewes nursing their lambs, or calves that have to nurse right now! The occasional black sheep are fascinating too and they *do* stand out. Like people, hmm?

The sheep have the right-of-way. Photo/Ellis Gravlin

NINE
My Life in the Broom Closet (Alias The 18-foot Trailer)

I had promised to keep my relatives and friends updated on the building project in Colorado, which I did, probably with more details than they wanted. As I wrote one of the progress reports, I was seated on a rock in a shady little glade overlooking the valley and the mountains.

In that progress report, I mentioned the Prayer to St. Joseph about selling the house, which came with the statue to be buried. Several friends requested a copy of it. I was impressed with it because no matter what your religious preference, it covers matters that should be of concern in any business dealing, not just selling property. Here it is:

> *To you, Blessed Joseph, we come with confidence in this our hour of need, trusting in Your powerful protection, Your loving service to the Virgin Mother of God and Your fatherly affection for the child Jesus. Inspire us with faith in the power of Your intercession before the throne of God. Lord, I've got some property I'd like to sell and I want to*

talk about it with You before I do. For myself, I ask that I'll be able to find a buyer and that I'll receive a fair price in exchange for this property. Help me to be honest in this sale, not to misrepresent the property value nor demand more than its worth. I pray also that the purchasers will put this to good use and it will not be abused nor neglected. Help all of us who become involved in this transaction to realize that all things are ultimately Yours and for Your service. Help us to willingly share our possessions with others who are in need. Grant that we may never be possessed by our possessions, but that we use them honestly and well in Your service. Amen.

Construction of the driveway and septic system had priority. The big backhoe took its first bite out of the mountain on Thursday, August 2. It was exciting to watch but there were lots of huge rocks underground. I tensed every one of my muscles in helping that backhoe break them up. The construction engineers did not have to blast, and while one operator dug up the earth, a smaller "cat" shoved it into position for a driveway. I was amazed at how quickly a rough drive was ready to use. The sloping drive led down to where the house would be built, with a garage underneath.

As is the way with most construction, the crew worked here awhile then hauled the big machinery away to other jobs. Everything halted while they waited for inspectors to okay each step of the septic field. Finally on August 18, the trailer was brought to the lot but until the water line and temporary electric pole were completed and inspected, it couldn't be used.

The water line was put in August 22 and because the original developer didn't blast to place the water main deep enough, the house line installers broke the main. Result: an impromptu shower and embarrassment for the workers who quickly recovered, repaired the main, and got the job done.

My house sitting for the Koskis ended when they returned on September 12. On the 13th I moved to the home of Mel and Nell

Thompson who lived across from my lot on Deer Ridge Drive. The Thompsons expected to be gone the entire week and I innocently thought I would be in the trailer by then. Hah! They graciously let me stay on and I was there a total of two weeks. I subsequently learned that when contractors or repairmen said they would be there Tuesday they neglected to specify *which* Tuesday, so I had to try to "divine" just when they *would* be there.

Rascal-cat spent the greater part of each day under the Thompsons' guest room bed and his nights in the basement. I took him out on the leash every day. He enjoyed it except when I restrained him from chasing the Thompsons' pet ground squirrels, chipmunks and mountain bluejays who came everyday for their free handout of peanuts. Nell had trained them well. One of the ground squirrels would take the peanut from her hand, and even from my unfamiliar one. It was such a thrill to feel that tiny paw as he rested it on my finger while taking the peanut! Later I fed them at the trailer but they were pretty wary of me for a while. When I told Rascal, "No! Those are pets," and held him back, he soon learned not to lunge toward them. He later respected that restriction up on the deck but on the ground it was a different matter. That was *his* territory.

One day on one of our leashed walks after we were in the trailer, I had an urgent need to return to it so I looped the leash handle over the trailer hitch. When I came back outside, Rascal had shrugged himself out of the harness and was gone! My heart dropped down into my stomach as I repeatedly called him. Then I decided I needed to alert the Thompsons in case he came that way. I trudged up the hill, a seemingly almost vertical 30 feet, and through huffing and puffing, told Nell what had happened. As we talked, she thought she heard him crying…and there he was, resting in a flowerbed. He walked slowly away from me but let me catch up to him and refasten the harness. I had to drag him almost the whole way back to the trailer. Another lost cat crisis was averted.

On the 25th, everything was hooked up for the trailer, with a drain to the septic tank. I came with Nell's bucket, rags, vacuum and other cleaning supplies. The trailer hadn't been used for two or three years and had a complete supply of dead flies in every nook and cranny. I scrubbed every inch of the inside. Mel and Nell supplied me with some dishes, an electric skillet and coffee pot, some bedding, towels, a small reading lamp, a small portable black & white TV and shelf space in their freezer to augment my tiny refrigerator. Koskis loaned some blankets and new friend Meredith Paschal came with pots, pans and cutlery. I was very grateful to all of them. I bought a few glasses and mugs to use along with borrowed dishes.

Here are a few things that happened within a short time: 1. Mel repaired a broken hot water hose twice, with the second break coming just as Nell stepped up to enter, drenching the lower part of her legs and shoes. 2. He restored electricity by jiggling the long extension cords running from the temporary pole. 3. The propane gas tank emptied and everything stopped. The builders/owners of the trailer brought me a larger tank. 4. About four days after Rascal and I moved in, the cold water line broke (flimsy plastic tubing) so the owners replaced it with copper tubing. 5. The pilot light on the gas oven went out periodically, resulting in long waits for the repairman. 6. The toilet bowl was cracked and a new one ordered but not yet received. In the meantime, I scrubbed the bathroom floor every time the toilet was used. That wasn't so bad because the entire bathroom was just a tad larger than a broom closet. Murphy lived with me – to strengthen my soul!

Let me describe the trailer. At one end was a couch of foam rubber cushions on a wood frame along the width, which made up into about a ¾-size bed when pulled out and the cushions were rearranged. It was hard to make up with regular sheets and I eventually bought a sleeping bag and skipped the sheets. There was storage above the couch area and a small chest of three drawers at one side. At the other end of the trailer was the dining booth, with a bunk area above which could also be slid out to take two small mattresses. I didn't pull it out but used half of the bunk space to store still unpacked boxes. The other half was claimed by Rascal as his refuge. He was up there a lot during the day when the construction workers weren't present but slept on my bed at night, keeping my feet warm.

I think the pattern name for the trailer tile was "Dirty Floor." The white background had specks of turquoise, pink, a little yellow and clever small brown dirt spots. Waxing helped a little.

In between the dining area and the couch on one side were the tiny sink, tiny counter space and small gas stove with cupboards above and under the sink, and three drawers. Opposite were a small closet, a tiny refrigerator with two drawers below and a cupboard above. Next to that, the gas heater and the bathroom with a shower hose much like those on many kitchen sinks. The entire room got wet when you showered. Quite an experience. My life-size poster of Tom Selleck hung on the bathroom door...the only space large enough. So, I happily shared the trailer with Tom Selleck! The poster was opposite the entrance door to the trailer and visitors were sometimes taken aback by what appeared to be a man standing there in that widow's abode.

Home to Rascal and me for four months. Photo/Boots

During those trailer/construction days, I met a number of Forest Lakes residents who included me in their plans. We visited Chaco Canyon in New Mexico (Pueblo Indian ruins) and the famed Mesa Verde ruins of an earlier group of Indians. New friends took me river rafting on the Animas River. We went to the Bar-D for Western Supper and the show several times. I visited Presbyterian churches in Bayfield and Durango, opting to join the nearer one in Bayfield.

As soon as possible, I took and passed my Colorado driver's license test and got new auto plates. They were much more expensive than in Illinois – $153, including a tax on the car which diminishes as the car ages. Like the good citizen I have always tried to be, I registered to vote.

I had a wonderful time playing Susie Homemaker as I selected appliances for the new house, and purchased at sale prices a dining room table, six chairs and a sofa bed that were held until I needed them. I even bought a pottery-base lamp at a moving sale, and stored it also with the Thompsons.

I continued to enjoy my early morning walks with Rascal, with hardly a thought of the pre-retirement days in Illinois. It was so still and peaceful. Deer Ridge Drive is on a cul de sac with little traffic since there were only two homes beyond mine. My frequent glimpses of deer always gave me a thrill – and still do.

TEN
"We" Build a House

Once the driveway and septic system had been completed and Rascal and I were ensconced in the trailer, I could turn my attention to house construction. This was my first venture into this kind of activity. I was so glad to be on the property where I wouldn't miss a thing. Maybe to the regret of the construction crew? No, not really. We had a very good relationship. It probably helped that I provided coffee and donuts or sweet rolls to everyone, me included, at break time. I felt as if they were all family. After a number of referrals to other lot owners, we still feel that way.

My lot is on the downhill side of the mountain with the result that both entrances to the house are at ground level – or nearly so on the upper level. Entrance there is by a ramp to accommodate David's wheelchair. This makes the upper view look as if it is a one-story house, but from both sides and the rear it is shown to be a two-story house.

Morrison Brothers Construction is headed by Greg and Paul who both looked much too young to have seven or eight children between them.

It was a wonderful crew – worked well together, no bad language – maybe the boom box was a little loud at times, probably to be heard over the noise of hammers and electric saws. To the regret of the Morrisons, who instructed the crew in vain, soda cans were sometimes just tossed aside by the younger workers, but picking them up gave me something to do once everyone had left for the day and Rascal and I made our inspection of the day's progress.

I took photographs of each step of the construction and sent copies of them to family and various friends so they could "see what I was up to." I was glad I had them years later when we had difficulty pinpointing a waterline leak. There in the photos were the several joints in the line, so the excavator doing the repair didn't need to dig up the entire yard but could zero in on the suspected spot. Consider this a word to every wise homeowner at construction time. It's fun to relive those days again through the pictures, because I loved every minute of it. From the other side of the memories, I even loved all those problems in the trailer.

Since I had never been involved in house building before, it was a special thrill to see them raise the walls that had been nailed together on the floor ahead of time. Voila! It begins to look like a house.

As construction progressed, I "helped" the contractor as owner to install the plumbing, thereby eliminating the need of a special contractor. My pictures prove it, showing me working on the trenches for the waterlines to be under the concrete and shoveling dirt over the pipes. Later, I also helped stain the woodwork and doors and painted a closet wall or two. In between my "tasks," I selected appliances and carpet and did other shopping for the house. I made charts for comparison shopping and looked for the best bargains, since I had plenty of time. Setting up a new household gave me a great deal of pleasure.

When the carpenters were ready to frame rooms, they asked if I wanted to make any changes on room dimensions. I did. I added a foot to the one-car garage that gave me a little more storage room, and on the upper level, I took a foot off my bedroom and added it to the small laundry room. Both decisions proved to be very good. When I began having overnight guests, I determined that I could have made one more beneficial change. I could have reduced the size of the large room on the lower level and added that space to the small bedroom. But it is still okay. The carpenters also let me decide how far apart to place the shelves in the pantry and laundry room cabinets.

Our first big snow of the season – eight inches – came in October. The house had progressed to the point where the rough floor on the upper level had been installed and was ready for framing. Now it was covered with snow. I dressed appropriately for the job and used one of their push brooms to push off the snow so it would at least be partially dry when the carpenters came to work.

Later that day, I was returning from a trip to Bayfield and started down my fairly long drive to park near the trailer. I was an innocent about driving on snowy, mountain roads and left the car in the drive gear, an opportunity for the car to give me a white-knuckle ride. Braking added to the thrill of swerving from side to side. I was just sure I would crash into the newly installed garage door! It was just dumb luck that an almost bare patch of ground let the brakes hold to get the car stopped. Whew! That was one well-learned lesson, and the last time I ever came down in drive gear when it was snowy.

Toward the end of November I asked Greg how come it was taking so long to finish the house. His reply, "Too long? We are almost finished and it has been only about three months! It usually takes five or six months." Then he went on to explain that it was going faster because I knew what I wanted so they didn't have to wait for me to make up my mind on some of the options. That came as a surprise to me but it did show my eagerness to get in and start "playing house."

The Certificate of Occupancy was granted by La Plata County on December 17, 1984, but since I was leaving the next day to spend Christmas in Florida, I stayed in the trailer again that night and moved into the house on my return, January 4, 1985.

During the summer I had purchased the living-dining room furniture, including two touch-on lamps, a new invention to me. My wonderful neighbors, the Thompsons, helped me move those items, stored in the garage until the house was completed, to the living level, along with the boxes I had packed dreamily back in Illinois.

Just prior to receiving the Certificate of Occupancy, I journeyed 70 miles to Cortez, Colorado, where my niece Diana and her husband Adolph lived, and purchased bedroom furniture. The store personnel loaded it all into Adolph's truck and when we returned to Forest Lakes, the three of us set it up.

Now I was all set. The appliances were already installed. It was beginning to look like a home!

On my return from the Christmas visit, I turned on the refrigerator and began to unpack boxes, put things away in drawers and cabinets (then later move them to a place I thought would be better) and just generally tried to get the feel of the place.

Early in the morning of the first night in my mountain home I was startled awake by a thumping noise coming from the kitchen area, which is close to the bedroom. Cautiously, I got up to investigate. As I stepped into the kitchen, the thumping noise began again. Then I laughed – it was the first ice cubes produced by the new refrigerator dropping into the storage bin.

The second early morning rude awakening came a few days later. It was a clatter that sounded like someone in cowboy boots stomping up the outside stairs to the deck. This time I pulled on a robe before peeking around the door frame to look toward the deck. If it was a cowboy, I wanted to be suitably covered. I saw nothing and ventured closer to the large windows overlooking the deck. Still nothing, so I unlocked the door and went out on the deck. Just below it was a very confused doe trying to decide in which direction she should flee. Later, Colorado natives told me my deck steps were probably right where a natural trail had been, so she clambered up the stairs, then back down again, still uncertain of this new development.

Strange noises and all, I really had fun "playing house."

Barb and David Nolan visit the new house Photo/Loren Dexter

ELEVEN
My New House in the Woods

To help you to geographically locate my new house in the woods I'll give you a few details. Forest Lakes is located about seven miles north of Bayfield on Highway 501, on the right. On the left is the Pine River Valley, defined by the Pine River and the highway. My house is about two miles from the development entrance and when it was first built, I directed visitors to it as "the first house on the right on Deer Ridge Drive." Now it is the sixth.

It is a two-level house, sited on the downward sloping lot to take advantage of passive solar power. The sun is directly above the house in the summer, but it shines into the south-facing windows in the winter. If I don't dampen down the wood stove by about 9 or 10 a.m. when the sun is shining, the room temperature soon reaches 90 degrees and I need to open the door or a window.

The upper level is the main living area. To the immediate left as you enter from the "street side door" which technically is the back door, is the bathroom with a sliding door to better accommodate a wheelchair. Directly across on the right is the laundry room. Next to that, also on the right, is the bedroom. Those doors all face a wide hall leading to a large kitchen with a built-in desk and a pantry on the right. A long counter on the left separates the kitchen from the dining/living "great room" that runs across the 24-foot width of the house.

Directly across from the counter on the south wall are two large stationary windows, each flanking a double expanse sliding door. Electric heat registers are permanently attached under each window, with wall space on each side. The windows on the east and west walls are in groupings of three and are a little shorter, giving wall space for furniture arrangement. All the windows combine to allow for solar heating in the winter and for a great panoramic view of woods, mountains, meadow and deep blue Colorado sky. On the living room side is a raised hearth and back wall of natural rock for the wood-burning stove. There is a cathedral ceiling of natural finish pine boards over the living/dining room, with vertical pine paneling on those walls. The sliding door leads to an 8 by 24-foot deck with a stairway to the ground.

Inside, the stairway to the lower level is on the west wall off the kitchen, leading to a large room with an outside door opening on a concrete patio under the upper-level deck. There is a closet, a smaller room with a big walk-in closet some visitors said you could put a baby's crib in, a wide hallway, a storeroom, another full bathroom and a doorway leading to the garage under the house.

I wasn't sure how this "city gal" was going to cope with a wood stove, but I knew that with back-up electric heat I wouldn't freeze if my fires fizzled out. It didn't take me too long to learn how to have a proper fire going. There is nothing, or almost nothing, as embracing as wood stove heat – like a hug from a loved one. A ceiling fan circulates the warmth. I regard chopping kindling, loading a large canvas bag with wood pieces on my airport luggage carrier, then trundling it down the ramp and into the living room near the stove or out on the deck for the wood holders as part of my winter exercise program. On really cold mornings I turn on the bathroom heater for a while but not in the other rooms. I need electric heat more in late spring and early fall before the days get and stay warm.

When it is time to replenish the wood supplies I ask my current cats if they want to help bring in the wood. Toro responds immediately but sometimes Miss Kitty needs a little prodding. Then she comes waddling to the door. Outside, they check in with me now and then for a vigorous rubdown with the leather gloves, and then pursue their inspection of the woodpile with its enticing scents of chipmunks, and the yard in general.

Most men seem to have a natural ability to fix the usual household things that break down, but in a male-less household, you learn to use various common tools or else put up with loose "whatevers." I have some talent for this but need much more on occasion. Because I don't abuse the privilege, my wonderful neighbors and now my nieces and nephews, have always been willing to apply their expertise or brute strength when needed. When son Rick comes, he brings my home up to snuff.

Sometimes guests insist on helping me with special projects. I don't demand it, you understand. And as good and versatile as any handyman when she comes to visit (often) is my friend Marian Gravlin. She has helped me paint the deck, the ramp and garage door, replaced screen sections in doors and caning in chairs, made curtains and replaced the vinyl on two chairs that came with a small kitchen set, purchased for $25 at the giant Forest Lakes Annual Yard Sale. We even stripped paint off the wood stove. The latter job became necessary because I used a stove polish that had wax in it which melted and peeled when a fire was lit. My nephew Tony later applied a new coat of paint.

In our painting adventures, Marian and I both learned (again) not to leave the paint can atop the ladder when moving the ladder. When I did it, the paint splashed on my blouse and then on the concrete patio. When Marian did it, the paint covered her chest, resulting in subsequent discarding of her entire wardrobe of the day. We have always been able to laugh at our foolish mistakes, and I hope that continues because there are sure to be more opportunities for mirth.

Our latest project during one of Marian's visits was to refurbish my wooden bear cutouts. The mama and her two cubs showed the effects of summer sun and the occasional rain over a period of several years. First we sanded, a quick job thanks to the loan of an electric sander from nephew Roger; then we applied a coat of primer paint. After that, we spray painted the bear family with an enamel coat. Wrong kind of paint – it wasn't compatible with the primer coat – it just powdered off. We trooped to Bayfield to buy brush-on enamel paint to give the bears an elegant black shiny appearance. A final application of accent paint for the noses, eyes and leg definition made them realistic enough for visitors to catch their collective breaths at first sight. The bears go into hibernation in my garage when the real creatures go to sleep for the winter.

Marian, right, and I refurbish the bears. Marian was wearing my paint-stained blouse from the earlier paint can atop the ladder caper. Photo/Roger Norris

Since 1999, two of my nieces and their husbands have built houses in Forest Lakes, and that pleases me to no end. My take on it is that the Lord has sent them to look after their ancient aunt in her old age! They are Emily and Roger Norris whose house is about a city block away down my street, and Anne and Tony Schrier who live higher up the mountain at about 8,000 feet. They are all of much help to me in many different ways – repairing, painting, electronic teachers, washing windows, shopping, etc. It may not seem like it to them but I *don't* present them with a "honey, do" list each time they come to visit.

One of the best house-warming gifts I received is the guest book. I ask visitors who come for a meal or overnight to sign it, including clubs or organizations that I entertain. It is really a historical record of who came when and how long they stayed. After 18 years of use, as of this writing, its pages have been taped in several places but it is wonderful for jogging the memory. *Was it three or four years ago that we had that surprise party?* As fast as time flies in retirement, a trip to the guest book shows it may have been five to seven years ago. It's also great for yielding names that don't want to stick in the mind. I highly recommend that every homeowner have a guest book because most people from away list addresses and sometimes phone numbers. And when you first move to the mountains, you have plenty of guests! Their comments reveal that visitors are especially impressed by the wildlife, the view, sometimes the food and the quietness at night.

Adjustments to being transplanted from the city to the mountains came in the form of a new vocabulary. I had to get used to *Avalanche Reports* along with statistics on snow depth at the ski resorts, moisture levels in an arid climate or the daily river flows, and learn the Spanish twist to names of towns and roads. For example: The village of Vallecito is not pronounced as it looks but is phonetically called *Vie-a-see-toe.* And Florida Road is not pronounced as the state is but *Flor-ee'-da.* I also got used to signs that declared the elevation of various cities and mountains.

TWELVE
My One-Acre "Spread"

I made the decision to leave the hillside yard natural, with no lawn to mow, precisely because it *is* on a hillside. The only large level spot is the septic field -- more properly called a Transfer Evaporation Field (TEF) – and the graveled parking area. I have gone through several lesser weed eaters because the tough clover plants eventually overpower the motors. I finally bought a bigger one to last longer but I don't last as long using it because it is heavier. Gas weed whackers are too heavy, so I struggle with joined outdoor extension cords. Where are those teenage kids who need a job? One neighbor girl helps me and she is a great worker. It is so satisfying to see a neat yard once the small areas of mountain grass and weeds are down.

When the TEF was installed, it included a large concrete tank with pipes leading from the house and a larger pipe at the other end where the broken down contents were released under the field. At that time (1984) an aerator was required under the Sanitation Code and was thought to be instrumental in breaking down the tank contents. The aerator was temperamental and ceased to work on occasion. At such times I had to press a reset button on the side of the house to restart it. A few years later when no amount of pushing the reset button brought results, I called the store where it was purchased and a representative came to look it over. He couldn't restart it either, and then told me they were no longer required in Colorado. Guess they must have been too much trouble for everyone. I just turned off the electricity to the aerator. Live and learn.

I established an important house rule right from the start: Don't put any pits or seeds in the garbage. Throw or plant them outside. The result: After a few years they grow, providing fodder for the deer, the chipmunks, ground squirrels and any other leaf-eating critters. And if they are persistent plants, I get fruit trees! After losing one that didn't transplant, I now have four producing peach trees. The crops have been bountiful most years so I can supply neighbors and friends and still have some for the freezer. And one year, a bear got most of them – but that unusual story is in the wildlife section. Can you wait? When some new homeowners checked with a nursery in Durango about planting peach trees, they were told it was too high here to grow them. My friends said, "Well, don't tell Boots that!"

One year a Durango friend (about 1,000 feet lower than my acreage) had a large crop of Bing cherries and shared some of them with me. I threw out lots of pits and buried some, too. One tough little tree kept trying each year but it could hardly grow because the deer regarded the fresh leaves as their personal salad bar. Finally it managed to get enough height to build on in the next year – and the next – until it was becoming a beautiful little tree, with some pruning help from a more knowledgeable neighbor than I. But it never produced blossoms. Some people told me I needed two trees, others said it needed to be grafted, but in the summer of 2001, there were blossoms on two branches on the east side of the tree. I was ecstatic! Cherry blossoms! I reveled in their beauty every day and when they faded, I kept checking to see if the cherries were setting up yet. One day I discovered that my cherry tree had ten tiny – *apples* – on it! O.K., a horticulturist I am not – I'll take the apples but I am watching a couple of other tiny trees, and will compare the leaves.

As a new mountain/forest landowner, I soon discovered one of the reasons they are named the Rocky Mountains. A pitchfork or shovel penetrates the earth about a half-inch, if you are lucky, and then you discover the rocks. I decided to put my flower plants in big pots scattered here and there, and they looked beautiful – for a few hours. Then the deer, the ground squirrels and other assorted critters thought they looked good, too – good enough to eat! When I asked a Forest Service employee what to plant to attract deer, he chuckled and said, "Anything you don't want them to eat."

After consulting with native experts, I made the decision to stick to daffodils, marigolds, columbine and wildflowers the animals don't like. A friend gave me starter plants of crown vetch, a spreading plant that highway engineers have found keeps their embankments in place. They have done their work well on my hillsides and have spread abundantly. The deer like to eat the lavender-pink blossoms on these but there is so much of it, they don't destroy it.

Beautiful in all seasons. Photo/Anne Schrier

THIRTEEN
Wildlife Watching

While still in the trailer, Rascal and I kept a sharp eye on the birds, deer, and chipmunks, and on the ground squirrels, which are larger, more rounded and have shorter tails than the chipmunks. Oh yes, and the unattractive rock squirrels that look like big rats with long slightly furry tails. In my opinion, God goofed on those and opossums in the good looks department. Rock squirrels are greedy and stuff their pouches with sunflower seeds, leaving none for the rest of the hungry ones unless I run them off. According to the genus name, it's O.K. to throw rocks at them, right? And according to that name they do have their burrows under the rocks, of which, as I mentioned before, there are aplenty in the Rocky Mountains. But don't fret – they are certain to be safe from tossed rocks, given my inexpertise at hurling.

The squirrels of preference are the Abert (broad A) squirrels, commonly called tassel-eared because the tops of their ears *do* sport tiny tassels. They have beautiful fluffy tails they arch over their backs while eating, creating a spectacular sight. Maybe they use their tails that way too in the rain but I haven't witnessed that. When several of them chase each other around on the deck their claws make a loud racket for such small creatures.

Young Abert squirrel, no tassels yet. Photo/Boots

The Abert squirrels are protected under Colorado law. Those maternal squirrels might need that protection if I can catch them in the act of raiding deck furniture cushions for soft fluffy stuff to line nests for their babies! During one early spring morning during my inspection of the deck I almost caught one of them but she scrabbled her way down the redwood house siding and up a nearby tree. In spite of my irritation about the torn chair cushion I had to laugh. There were white gobs of polyester stuffing protruding from each side of her mouth. I hope the babies enjoyed it because some of that damage is hard to repair.

Living alone, it is my practice to read while I eat (my companionship). My dining room table is placed to offer a good view of deck activities. One day while eating lunch, I was reading a *Reader's Digest* condensed book featuring a story about the Lewis and Clark Expedition. I was startled – and thrilled – to learn that many of the very birds and animals I saw on my deck – Clark's nutcracker, Lewis woodpecker, Cassin's finch, Steller's jay, Abert squirrel – were named by and after members of the expedition. Following advice of others who have lived in the Rockies for a while, the first time I see a new critter or bird, I look it up in my bird or wildlife book and circle the entry, noting the date first observed. My Peterson's *Guide to Western Birds* is precious and well thumbed. The birds noted include Cassin's, gold, rosy and red crossbill finches; chickadees; nut hatches; pigmy nuthatches; pine siskins; Steller's; pinon and gray jays; juncos; Clark's nutcrackers; evening and black-headed grosbeaks; downy, hairy and Lewis woodpeckers; hummingbirds; hawks; ravens; crows; occasionally sharp-tailed grouse, flycatchers, cowbirds, eagles, western tanagers; and once, a peregrine falcon passing through.

Experience taught me the best locations for hanging various bird feeders. Some of the first ones were suspended from brackets attached to roof support poles on the deck but this resulted in many bird droppings on the railings. In my eagerness to keep my new house looking as attractive as possible, I was out on the deck scrubbing the railings every day. But one day I thought, *wait a minute – this isn't why you retired!* Now I clean them periodically, or let rain and snow do the job. On a visit nephew Craig Holt and his colleague Bob Marrero installed a PCB pipe extending outside the railing. I can swing the suspended feeder toward me for filling and then secure it. The bird droppings fall to the ground.

It's always a thrill to see deer in singles, or with fawns or yearlings traveling in packs of several does and bucks munching on my plant goodies. Old timers in the area as well as newcomers drop everything and watch. I don't consider it time wasted even though some household tasks may go un-done for a while. I keep a salt lick down in the woods below the house for the deer. Their tongues create fascinating canyons and crevasses in the 25-pound block. When my friend Marian was visiting one July, we purchased a new salt lick and decided to deliver it to the area with my little red wagon instead of trying to carry it down with our arthritic fingers. The wagon reacted to the gravity of the hillside and tipped over. The salt lick rolled way down past the spot where it should have come to rest. It must have been a laughable sight as Marian and I rolled that heavy thing back up the hill to where it belonged, but we got it there.

One summer I was drawn to the window by a rather strange noise that sounded a little like a French horn with a beginning player at the mouthpiece. For some time I was entranced by the sight of a grown buck teaching a young buck sprouting new antlers how to use them against foe. It was the young buck making the strange sounds. When they moved off the septic field-boxing ring, they wandered up the hill across from my house and resumed the sparring.

Look carefully! There are two deer there. Photo/Boots

Hollyhock leaves and blossoms must be especially tasty to deer. If one of those plants manages to survive to the blossom stage it is rare. And if it does, I count myself lucky. I looked out the door one day and found a doe munching on the top part of a stem that she had broken off. I laughed, for she looked just like the opera character, Carmen. Instead of a rose between her teeth, the doe was systematically sending the stalk with red blossoms through her mouth, obviously enjoying her hollyhock find.

It is not unusual when checking on the status of growing

hollyhocks to find nothing but a few stems left by a marauding band of deer. Sometimes they come through the yard in groups of two to seven or eight deer – does, fawns, yearlings and bucks. Even when they are plucking peaches from my volunteer trees, they are a thrill to see. The fawns are spotted for most of their first year, sporting a "summer tan" that blends in with the color of the rocks. Late in the fall, the coats turn a dark tree trunk color to aid in their camouflage.

I have even made up a little love song to sing softly to them. Most often they stand there, seemingly entranced, watching me. Or maybe they are thinking, "What's with her?" I prefer to describe them as being spellbound – before they move on.

For several years I have observed a deer I dubbed *Lonesome Doe*. Apparently she has never given birth to a fawn and maybe for that reason, the other deer families reject her. When she tries to join them, they run her off but in my human interpretation of the snub, I think she looks at the group of them somewhat wistfully. She comes through the yard frequently, trimming the crown vetch and sampling anything else that looks good to her. But she is always alone.

I don't think I am so wrong about attaching human reactions to animals. They are sensitive and maybe they are sometimes sent by God to offer comfort in a time of anxiety. When my grandson, Tony, was about 17 he had his second open-heart surgery to have a valve replacement and I was concerned. From childhood he had an affinity for deer. On the morning of the operation, a doe lay down unusually close to the house entrance, chewing her cud and resting. When I got the call that the operation was over and was successful, she left. Coincidence? I doubt it.

A mama skunk has reared her young ones under my concrete patio for several years. No, there is no odor from there although the night hours sometimes bring odors from visiting skunks. To date, my cats have not been sprayed and it may be because skunks are also considered part of the cat family. When the cats were still kittens, they started after mama skunk one day when she left the nursery, with me up on the deck waving my arms and beseeching them not to follow her. She was faster than they were so they soon lost interest, to my relief.

The skunks all look so soft and velvety but a binocular-view shows the fur to be rather coarse. One year my favorite little one had unusually long back legs so he looked as if he were leaning forward all the time. When the cats were let out onto the patio, they all ignored each other so I quit worrying about encounters. For the past several years there has not been a family under the patio and I think it's because the ugly rock squirrels have commandeered the space. I don't consider that a fair exchange!

New construction in the area has apparently discouraged some of the wildlife from coming around. In my early years in the woods I occasionally saw foxes and some years saw a line of wild turkey mamas and their poults marching around the property, eating the hen scratch I had scattered, bought especially for them. I have seen mountain lion tracks in the snow but not the creatures. Generally speaking, they are wary of humans and try to avoid them. They are more likely to be active during the night or early morning hours but if I venture out into the night I turn on the light and look all around for any creatures.

The first time I saw a bear near my house it was about 1:30 in the afternoon. I had been whacking down the weeds, not a quiet activity, when I decided to break for lunch. As I approached the ramp to the house, I was noisily calling to the cats because I hadn't seen them in a while. I looked up and saw a shiny black bear about 50 feet away, heading up the hill on the lot next door. He (?) paid no attention to me and continued toward a large stump, sniffed around it for a few minutes, then headed east through the woods. I frantically called the cats then but they didn't respond. They probably had been in hiding long before I spotted the bear! Eventually they came to the door to be let in. Before that, I ran to the phone to alert my neighbors to the east of the bear headed their way. Having to leave a message on their answering machine wasn't too satisfactory but at least I knew they weren't in immediate danger if they weren't home.

My next bear sighting came several years later at 4:30 one September afternoon in 1999, a year that was unusually dry and lacking in the usual "bear food." I was casually leaning on the deck railing, being grateful again for the beauty that surrounds me, when I saw movement down below near the peach trees. A bear was standing upright reaching for a peach. The fruit was not at all ripe and was rock hard but he pulled one off and ate it anyway. I quietly went into the house for my camera, hoping he would wait for me. He was still there and obliged me by sticking around while I took several pictures. I knew they would only be so-so because I was aiming into a setting sun. The only alternative would be for me to go down the steps to ground level – which I was not about to do! He feasted for a while and then ambled across the septic field and into the woods. I later found a great number of half-eaten green peaches and a few bare pits on the ground around the trees.

Typical of the bears in Forest Lakes. Photo/Roger Norris

Since my Colorado adventure began, my Christmas letters to friends and relatives primarily have been updates on what's going on in my life. I have threatened to discontinue that practice several times but each time I am assured that they don't want to be dropped from my list. So here is an excerpt from the 1999 letter regarding my next experience with a bear that came a month later:

I swear I am not a nut case, but one of my big thrills in 1999 was a spiritual connection with a big, brown cinnamon bear on my ramp, about 6 feet from my door. He (?) had been eating my still-green peaches for a week or so, breaking branches in the process. A late spring frost made fruits, berries and acorns scarce for hungry bears. He had already decimated the choke cherry tree and worn a path through the Crown Vetch plants.

My cats alerted me to his presence at 6:15 one morning so I turned on the outside light. There he was, upright, in a casual pose with his big right paw resting on the railing. Nothing aggressive in his expression, which was apologetic, if anything, for eating my peaches, which he needed to hibernate. I mentally told him it was o.k. and picked up my camera. We continued to study each other, with absolutely no fear on either side. I'll never forget his face. It was hard to film him through the diamond-shaped glass so I decided to open the inner door (screen in place). He did not react to the slight click of the deadbolt nor the open door, so I took a few shots, but the aluminum screen just threw back the light and I didn't get a picture (detailed photos of the tiny screen squares, though!). Then he turned and slowly went back up the ramp and outside the circle of light. But we communicated! Truly, we did!

In the summer of 2001, I saw one on my deck at 10:30 one night, which I thought at first was a huge, shaggy dog with some gray hairs in the fur, checking out the seed pan. When he lifted his head and I saw him in profile I knew it was an old bear. I banged on the sliding glass door and screeched and he moved to the head of the stairs, looking over a bird feeder and the hummingbird feeder before he went down the steps. He probably thought this restaurant was too noisy or he may have been deaf. Then I brought in the feeders for a few nights but when there was no return visit, I started leaving them out – until two weeks later, when a marauder ruined a seed feeder, demolished the hummingbird feeder and ran off with the suet holder. What feeders remained, spent the nights inside until the bears were in hibernation.

With the continued drought in the Southwest, we have bears coming down from the high country in search of food. They are quite adept at getting around the efforts of humans to keep them from garbage cans, etc. One woman told me her husband had strong chains holding down the lid of their large can but a huge bear just picked it up, squeezed it in the middle and the lid popped off! He daintily pulled each item out of the can separately for a leisurely meal.

Fruit tree profiles change rapidly when bears climb them, searching for whatever is there, ripe or not. Broken branches need to be trimmed after each visit. One medium-sized bear had already done his work on my young apple tree when I spotted him coming back to my yard again. He was looking over the tree. I was up on the deck looking down at him and informed him that he was an idiot for breaking branches because then there would be no fruit the next year. He heard me but just went on his way, checking out a peach tree that had already been picked clean.

That night, the same bear (I think) was on my deck. Miss Kitty alerted me again that something was out there. I turned on the light and at first didn't see him, then he moved and I discovered he was up on the railing (2 by 4). He traveled the length of it (24 feet), examining the feeder hardware along the way, then coming back again. He was very agile as he made his way around the support posts, bracing one leg on the inside of the post and moving around the post to the next section of the railing. Finding nothing, he came down and headed for the wide windowsill but the seeds that had been there had fed the birds. My heart was in my mouth for a few seconds when he stood, stretching his front paws up high on the window. I later realized he was checking out the sun catcher angel that was hanging on the inside of the window. They do sometimes break windows. Could he have come through this double-paned one? Perhaps, but he didn't try, luckily for me.

Next, he began eyeing the wind chime. I was inside observing all of this and thought, *surely he doesn't think that's food!* He stood upright again and swiped at it, breaking two of the chains and pulling off a hummingbird ornament. Now I have to repair that.

From the safety of the house, I watched one bear bend down the supple trunk of an ornamental crab apple tree so he could eat the few withered apples and leaves. The tree got away from him a couple of times, springing upright, but the third time he pulled it down, he put his body across it, holding it down until he finished eating. A few days later, nephew Roger brought a metal post and wire to pull the trunk to an upright position. I have no doubts that if the bear returns again next year, he will easily twist the wire to his purpose.

So, until the drought ends and berries and acorns are again plentiful in the high country, we will have bear invasions at the lower altitudes. In Colorado, we can be fined for feeding the bears. I don't do that intentionally but I can't help it when they invade the fruit trees. I can remove the bird feeders at night, which I do until they go into hibernation. "Living With Wildlife" posters and newspaper articles advise us during bear season on what to do and not do if we encounter one. I have been chastised for opening the inner door to my spiritual bear but if he had been aggressive, probably neither the screen door nor the wooden door would have stopped him.

A continuing featured attraction on the deck for guests and me is the masked bandit family. I buy fifty-pound bags of #2 raw peanuts in the shell (especially for feeding wildlife), and sunflower seeds, preferably in 50-pound bags, but they really don't last too long. Except for a couple of downtimes for birds, the seeds only last about two weeks. The peanuts last two or three months. I think my road to the poor house will be paved with receipts for the purchase of sunflower seeds and peanuts!

The raccoons discovered both were pretty good eating so they became regular nighttime visitors. I line the wide windowsills on the deck with the "goodies," but don't try to make pets of the visitors. Even now, they scamper off the deck if I open the door. The real fun began when mama raccoon first brought her little ones along so they could feast too. There were three babies in the first contingent, usually there are four and once she had five babies in tow. They are little balls of gray fluff with masks and striped tails. It is the same mother, identified by a small nick in one ear.

Licking her sticky paw. Photo/Ellis Gravlin

My heart beats wildly when the little ones, who can hardly make the reach from one horizontal railing to the next, scrabble for a clawed foothold to climb to the top of the railing. A misstep can send them onto the rocks below. I really bit my nails when mom was raiding the hummingbird feeder attached to an upright post, with three little ones up there with her trying to nurse! She was pretty clever when the fluid level got low in the feeder. She set up a slight swinging motion and when it came back to her, she drank it.

I don't fasten the feeders where raccoons can reach them anymore. They wrecked too many of them. My late friend Ellis Gravlin took one of my prized photos of that drinking operation. He put the camera lens directly on the window so there was no glare. My title for that picture is "Who says there is no free lunch?"

One summer evening the cats were lounging around on the floor and I was reading/watching television – I always have a paper, magazine or book in my lap to use during commercials or less than interesting programs – when one of the cats produced a loud unusual growl. I got up to investigate and found them "pointing" at the deck door. The cats had stopped reacting to every raccoon that appeared on the deck some time ago but this was something new.

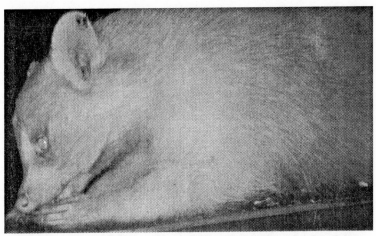

**On the windowsill. The eyes are pink and the fur is white.
Photo/Boots**

On the other side of the door was an albino raccoon, which the cats did not recognize as belonging to the raccoon family. And no wonder! Without the traditional mask and striped tail, he looked like a huge pink-eyed rat with a fluffy tail. The growling didn't stifle the raccoon's curiosity about the cats on the other side of the screen door and he looked them over before returning to his sunflower seed meal in the dish.

I wondered what would happen if he came when the "regulars" were on the deck. Would they reject him as the cats did? The question was soon answered. Most of them paid no attention to him but one played with him and shared the seed dish. I have described the albino raccoon as "he," but more likely it was a female, or at least regarded as no threat by mama raccoon who would not let her siblings or members of her past broods bring their families up to "her" deck.

There was a departure from that practice a couple of years ago when one of her brood fell from the railing onto the rocks below. A day or so later I noticed she was limping and one back foot was obviously injured. Apparently it hurt her to stand on it so she lay down on her stomach to munch on the seeds in the dish. Still does that now and then. The mother (nicked ear) permitted the injured offspring to remain with her during the winter and on into the next season. As was mom's custom, she produced three more babies. Usually I was aware of them in June when I found a tipped-over water dish, or muddy water as they played or sat in it, or toppled plants. Sometimes the "aunt" was with them. The babies were not brought up to the deck until they could negotiate the steps. One night in early September I was aware of more than the usual racket on the deck and turned on the light to investigate. There was the injured one with *four* babies! Never before had I seen babies produced that late in the season. Another batch of little balls of fluff with masks and striped tails. Because they were so young, I hoped the winter wouldn't be too hard on them. I think raccoons spend part of the winter in semi-hibernation because they don't come to the deck every night.

I don't know for sure how many years that raccoon brought her family to our deck (hers and mine) but it has to be at least seven years and could be longer than that. I haven't seen that old mother for two years and I miss her, but that's the way of the cycle of life. I am grateful to the Lord and appreciative of all His bounty that comes my way. He surrounds me with beauty, birds and animals that bring humor and awe into my life.

FOURTEEN
Not Exactly Wildlife

A year or so after my home was built, Ed Wommer, a rancher friend whose family I had come to know at church, told me he had a cow ready to calve. As a city girl I had never seen a calf born so I asked if I could come to watch when the time came. He probably thought I was a little off base but agreed to call me if that was what I really wanted. I did, and he did, directing me to drive my car right out into the pasture where the cow was. I stayed back far enough not to alarm her and proceeded to get educated. In my excitement to get to the ranch just down the highway from Forest Lakes, I neglected to take binoculars and camera. Oh well, I was sure I would remember it to relate to others later. It was far different from the many kitten births I had played midwife to down through the years.

The cow's contractions were visible, and she was restless, lying down for a while, then getting up to pace, and repeating the process. She was a little way off from the rest of the herd – maybe they were respecting her privacy. Finally she got up and in a very determined fashion swung her rear end around until the calf slid out. The little bull calf lay there quite awhile in exhaustion while I worried if he was still alive. Mom licked him periodically and then he struggled to his feet. Her strong licking knocked him down again but he persevered until he was walking around, and then headed instinctively for the "buffet table." I could relax. He was going to be all right.

A few days later the rancher called me with the news that this one was going to be a breech birth. I hurried to the scene, again without camera or binoculars (my learning retention was not very high). I was led into a barn where the cow was already secured in a stanchion. My friend and a ranch hand fastened a chain around the legs of the calf, which were already part way out of the birth canal. Then to my horror they applied a winch and proceeded to stand and jump up and down on the chain! This was not my idea of a birthing!

As the rancher knew it would be, the calf was finally pulled all the way out and he dragged the newborn out of the barn through the dirt. The cow was released and led out to the calf where she proceeded to clean him up. I can just imagine her thinking, when she encountered all the dirt on him: *Where the heck has this kid been?*

I witnessed one more birth that spring but this one came off with a minimum of fuss and in timely fashion. And I never got one picture!

Little babies of any species have a certain charm and these were no exceptions. I was glad to have the experiences, even if they weren't wildlife in the strictest sense of the word.

FIFTEEN
The Feline Follies

Three cats have shared my mountain home during these years. If you have lived with cats you will identify with many of the episodes. There may even be parallels if dogs are your companions. Some of my friends are "dog people" and frequently tell me of similar stories of life with their beloved pets. We commiserate with each other when disaster strikes them or when a pet has to be put down. We unashamedly take advantage of the many sympathy cards on the market for just such occasions. Whether they are dogs or cats, these members of our households make our lives richer and we wouldn't be without them.

Rascal-cat adapted readily to life in the woods. Maybe it was an instinctive and vague memory of kinship to jungle animals like lions, panthers and cheetahs. His main occupation was terrorizing the chipmunks and birds at first. I did manage to train him to leave the birds on the deck alone but the ground was *his* domain and my words were not heeded. Sometimes he would be lying on a mat on the deck about three feet away from a dish where the birds were feeding. He would just watch them, after first looking into the house to see if I was watching him, and if so, would leave them alone. Then it became customary for him to ignore them.

One day, he was sleeping there when a young evening grosbeak, who had not yet learned where danger lay, hopped onto Rascal's tail. The cat's head jerked up which sent the bird flying away. Rascal looked around for a moment then went back to sleep. My turn with a bird on the deck came when I was reading on the lounge chair, with my knees up. Apparently I had been quiet enough with my page turning that I was regarded as part of the furniture. A young bird – an evening grosbeak again – landed on my knee, startling both of us, but I enjoyed it..

When we were still in the trailer I took Rascal for walks on a leash and those walks were challenges to me because he would go under logs, with me pleading to "Wait!…wait for me!" while I maneuvered the leash to the other side. The first time he really got his freedom came while I was reading, sitting on a low stool outside the trailer with Rascal on the leash and the handle secured under a stool leg. Out of the corner of my eye I saw him struggling and shrugging to free himself from the body harness. I decided this was the time of trial and watched him get free of the leash. I let him go and he wandered off to explore on his own. Nervous "Mom" watched until he was no longer visible then I went inside the trailer, eyes searching from window to window. No sighting. Imagining all the terrible things that could be happening to him. Even in daylight, I didn't know what dangers the woods held. I worried until I heard him meow outside the trailer door to come in. We had both passed the test.

During construction, when the crew arrived, he ran to the closet and frantically waited for me to open the door. He recognized the sounds of all the trucks, and he stayed in the closet until the last truck left and I told him it was all right to come out now. Which he did promptly.

In the summer after moving into the house, Rascal climbed way up in a very tall pine tree. There was no way I could get him down by cajoling, urging, commanding or nearly crying. Finally I told him he was on his own and went in the house. Before long he came sauntering across the deck to the door as if he hadn't spent the past four or five hours high up in a tree.

About a year after landing in Colorado, Rascal developed diabetes. I was suspicious when I recognized the same symptoms that people indicate – excessive thirst and frequent urination. My beloved veterinarian, Dr. Jerry Brown, confirmed the diagnosis and said I would have to give him a daily insulin shot. Me? Give him shots? Yes! I learned!

Because I would have to test the insulin level in his urine, I had to keep him from the litter box during the night so I shut the door to the laundry room, AKA Rascal's rest room. Then the trick was to teach him to wake me if he couldn't hold it any longer – and that *was* a trick. He always slept on my bed but only once did I have to respond to a slowly spreading warmth to my body. I changed the bedding in the middle of the night, leaving the washing until daylight. The following night he chose a spot next to the bathtub. In the morning I picked him up and let him smell that spot, telling him, "No, No!" Then I carried him to my bed, repeating the admonition and took him to the litter box, scratching in it a little. He was a smart cat! I only had to do that two or three times before he got the message.

He figured out his own method of waking me up. Usually, around 5 or 6 a.m. he gently batted at my face with sheathed claws, or sometimes by biting my hair. I had the testing material and a watch with a second hand next to the litter box. When I opened the laundry room door, he climbed into the box and even let me lift his tail a little so I could see to place the diagnostic stick under the stream. That determined how much insulin he would need after his morning meal. Later on, improvements to the insulin made the timing unnecessary so it was somewhat easier. After that ritual, both of us went back to sleep.

Based on information from the diagnostic stick, I prepared the needle with the proper amount of insulin for the injection and had a cotton swab and alcohol ready for cleaning the area. I was to give the shots on the right, left and middle of his back in the shoulder area, alternating each day. He didn't run from me when he knew what was coming and let me lift him to the bathroom vanity where everything was in readiness. Dr. Brown said the needle could be used several times and returned to the antiseptic container after each use. Rascal only protested when the needle became a little dull – then he yowled and scowled at me while I apologized.

We both learned how to do it! Photo/Jim Schneider

His first experience with an insulin reaction nearly scared me to death. I was eating lunch, Rascal resting in a chair, when he gave a strange cry and tried to stand up on trembling legs, falling back into the chair. An immediate call to the vet, nine miles away, yielded instructions to bring him in pronto. I got him into the big cage in the car but couldn't see him from the driver's seat and because he was silent on the trip, I almost had him dead and buried before he emitted a cry at the first stop sign. What a relief! After that when I used the cage, it was placed on the front seat.

Dr. Brown administered a 50% Karo Syrup/water solution to Rascal orally while an aide, with me watching anxiously, shaved a front leg to prepare it for a tube insertion to give him glucose. He came around from the syrup solution, so the tube wasn't necessary. On subsequent insulin reactions, Rascal always let me know with that distinctive cry and I prepared the solution immediately. He didn't like to have the syrup injected into his mouth from a small syringe, so one day in exasperation I pushed the little custard cup with the syrup in it in front of him and commanded him to drink it himself! Which he did, and which I continued to do when the solution was needed again.

Rascal-cat lived almost four years with the disease, about three months shy of his 17th birthday, longer than Dr. Brown expected. The day came when I had to make the decision to end his life, and that was very difficult. He was having too many problems. He had lost bladder control – embarrassing to tidy cats – couldn't eat and couldn't stand. The last time he was outside and able to come in by himself he left a muddy paw print on the doorsill. I preserved it by spraying it with clear polyurethane. It's still there.

Rascal was silent on that last trip to see Dr. Brown, but I wasn't. I told that dear cat how much I loved him and recounted all the good times we experienced together, especially at our little house in the woods. Dr. Brown asked if I wanted to wait outside the examining room while the deed was done. I refused, and continued to talk to Rascal with my head down near his. It's a wonder Dr. Brown didn't get the shot in me, but he didn't, and pretty soon Rascal's little head slowly lowered to the table and it was over. I cried, Dr. Brown cried and hugged me. His wet-eyed assistant placed Rascal in a plastic bag and I left for home, crying and driving. My good friend Loren Dexter came and dug the grave in Rascal's beloved woods below the house, not an easy task in these mountains. Loren secured in the dirt a flat upright rock tombstone on which he later painted a black cat and the dates, 7-3-72 to 3-27-89.

About two weeks after Rascal's euthanasia, Dr. Brown came over to me after church, put his arm around me and asked how I was doing. Of course, I started to cry and said I still wondered if I had done the right thing. He emphatically assured me that I had and that helped a little bit.

Eleven months later, in February, I noticed huge footprints in the snow down below the deck going away from the house. *Human?* I wondered. I put on my winter gear and set out to identify them and see where they led. When I got close enough, it was easy to attribute them to a bear. My wild animal book agreed with me.

Stepping beside the tracks, I followed them to Rascal's gravesite, where I found the pink towel I had wrapped him in, and bits of bone and fur. I replaced them in the grave. Two months later in another part of the woods I found Rascal's skull, identifiable by a missing incisor tooth on one side. I returned that to the grave too and piled more rocks on it. The bears normally wouldn't be out of hibernation in February but we had an unusually warm spell that year and coupled with a very dry fall and winter, the ground was more sandy than solid. That made it easier for the bear to dig into the grave. I was incensed at first, then realized that Rascal's spirit wasn't there – *but I still didn't want that grave disturbed.*

He was my good companion and his last three and a half plus years with diabetes made us very close. I know he enjoyed that time roaming the woods, stalking little creatures in the way nature intended. I still miss him even though two more cats later came to share my life.

One day in August, about two and a half years after the loss of Rascal, I went to the grocery store in Durango to get some of Colorado's wonderful Olathe corn on the cob. There were two young kids with a box in front of the store. I glanced in as I usually do in those situations and saw three kittens. One of the kids quickly told me the little gray one was spoken for. Of the remaining two, one was black with a little coloration and the other was tan with black and brown stripes. In less than a second I said, "I'll take the other two." *Where did that come from?* No pondering the decision, just "I'll take them." The kids said they would keep them for me while I finished shopping for the corn – and for cat food and cat litter that were not on my list of chores for the day. The store provided a box with fairly high sides for transporting the three-month-old lively ones. I managed to push them back to the bottom of the box while driving as they repeatedly tried to climb out. Because of a vigilant guardian angel, we got home safely.

My new friends didn't get their names for a few days as I wanted to see if any special personality traits would emerge. They were not from the same litter but came from neighboring farms. Because she was small and dainty and very feminine, "Miss Kitty" was so dubbed. She is a tri-color tabby, mostly black but with some ivory, orange and gold showing through, and one ivory-colored foot competing with three black ones. She also has quite a bit of Siamese in her lineage, evidenced by the innocent wide-eyed look she gives me with her big green eyes as she ignores instructions. Alas, she is no longer tiny and dainty, partly owing to her habit of finishing Toro's food when he grazes, intending to return to it later.

In their kitten friskiness, both Miss Kitty and Toro tore through the house, challenging everything in their paths. But Toro was particularly boisterous. El Toro was so named because he was born in May, Taurus on the Zodiac sign, and was like a bull in a china shop. As a kitten he charged into a room, leaped up on an end table, scattered everything on it – sometimes even the lamp – knocked off sofa cushions and left the room a disaster area. And yet he delicately leaps from floor to counter to refrigerator to the top of the cabinets where it is warm to sleep in winter and he lies down among precious breakables. Some are now moved to a safer area. I didn't put things up for my children but these cats are another matter. Sometimes Toro leaps directly from countertop to the top of the cabinet while I watch warily. He has always made it – so far – as he ages. Miss Kitty used to make that leap but now she is too fat.

Toro is a tiger-striped tabby with velvety brown and/or black stripes on tan-gold-white-gray fur. He has four white feet and a white bib and ruff around his neck that he keeps sparkling clean. He has little tufts of hair at the top of and in his ears, suggestive of a Maine Coon cat. I must confess that while I was pondering names and finally settled on Miss Kitty for the obvious reasons, I considered a little alliteration in naming Toro. He was such an attractive kitten, that Mr. Pretty came to mind until I mentioned it to my daughter, who was horrified that I would give that name to a male cat. Did I overreact by giving him the Spanish name for "The Bull"?

They had been outside cats so I figured they would need to be trained to use the litter box. I picked up Miss Kitty and carried her to the litter box. Holding her paw, I made scratching motions while she struggled mightily to get down. I persisted for a while and then released her. She immediately stepped into the box for a superb performance. When I repeated the actions with Toro, he also struggled with determined force but when he was released from my grip, he fled the laundry room. It was with relief later when I watched him march into the room and prove to me that he knew what it was for. The only time solids appear outside the box is when I delay for too long before replacing the litter or when their covering up activities are too forceful. So *they* have trained *me*.

Once they were big enough to jump to the stools at the counter between the kitchen and dining room and then to the counter, the fun began. They discovered that wrapped candy in the dish made excellent hockey pucks they could bat far into the surrounding rooms and down the stairs. It makes for pretty weak discipline when I am laughing at their antics. One night they found a new hockey puck when I left my hearing aids on the bathroom counter. I found one of the aids down on the lower level, but it survived the trip down the steps. Now the aids are safely stashed in a drawer overnight.

The cats have further trained me to permit them to be on the counter. I just make sure I don't leave food on it – and scrub the countertops frequently – especially when guests are coming. I understand why they like to be up on the countertop. That way they have unlimited views out of all the windows which they can't see from the floor when the doors are closed. And besides, they live here too – that's why I sometimes sit in a different chair than intended when I find it occupied by one or both of them. I guess I *am* well trained.

I *have* trained them to a couple of things – by accident, I guess. When they were new to me, I sat down in the living room to eat some ice cream one evening and they were both on my lap in an instant. I moved the dish away from their eager mouths, saying firmly, "Mine!" And it worked, to my surprise. It helps to give them their treat before I settle down to mine. I still use that word and no-nonsense tone now and then. And they still obey it. My other training victory is to get them to move when they are in the way by saying, "Toot, Toot!" – and they move.

Miss Kitty was spayed at age six months and recovered rapidly, running through the house chasing El Toro two days later. It was Toro's turn two months after that and he took it in stride. I breathed a sigh of relief – safe at last.

They wage mock battles accompanied by a vicious sound track of howls and hisses, leaving fur tufts on the floor, complete with pounding feet that make an incredible amount of noise on the carpeting.

Maybe it is an instinctive maternal urging, even though she is now an "it," but Miss Kitty is very protective of Toro if she thinks he has been hurt or is threatened. If I accidentally step on Toro's tail, she is right there looking over the situation when she hears his cry.

It was soon apparent by horrible breath that they each had bad teeth and gums – their moms' poor pregnancy diet maybe? Eventually Dr. Brown pulled six teeth from each of them and prescribed antibiotics I had to administer. Yes, they had a few teeth left and soon learned to gum even the hard food. Miss Kitty accepted her dosages, squirted into her mouth, with a minimum of fuss, but Toro struggled and howled in a loud voice. I struggled with Toro, and with Miss Kitty who clawed at my leg to get me to stop mistreating him! At least enough of the medicine got to its destination to get the healing job done – and no more teeth have been extracted.

I have never seen cats that showed so much interest in the type of shoes I am wearing, especially if they are different from my usual footwear. They watch my feet intently and seem fascinated by the occasional higher heels. Maybe they recognize them as potential disaster.

If you have observed cats in your household or when visiting "cat houses" you probably have noticed that when a paper, book, clothing or any flat object is put down, a cat will immediately inspect and stretch out on it. One day I broke down a cardboard box, intending to use it to start a fire in my wood stove. I dropped it to the floor while I tended to the stove. Miss Kitty promptly claimed it as her own. I didn't have the heart to dislodge her and used newspapers for the fire. Through some form of communication they took turns lying on it, with the other cat nearby. It was used often. The cardboard was getting tattered so when I was expecting a guest, I decided to get rid of it. As I picked it up, I caught sight of Miss Kitty, her eyes big with alarm. Her concern was so evident that I just slid the treasured cardboard under the couch until the guest left. She still looked upset until the approaching stranger caused her to flee to safety. I dragged it out when the coast was clear and the cats enjoyed it until I *did* burn it in the last fire of the season. Maybe it was the combination of the cardboard next to the fire but they didn't seem to miss it when they could lie in front of the screen door in warm weather.

As I mentioned earlier, when they were still quite small, they would come running into a room and up on whatever piece of furniture offered them a challenge. This included the bed, toilet seats, chairs, the couch and desk if there was something close by they could jump on first.

Toro got more than he bargained for one day when I was cleaning on the lower level in preparation for houseguests. He came charging down the hall, into the bathroom and up on what he assumed was the usual position of the toilet seat. Instead, he jumped into the toilet bowl where I had just put the blue cleaning liquid. He and I were both in a panic. I snatched him up and held him in the sink, running cool water over his bedraggled body. I didn't know how much damage the solution could do to his skin and fur. He went into his usual howling and struggling during the rinsing process, which brought Miss Kitty on the run to protect him through her leg-clawing routine. It's a good thing I usually had on long pants during these encounters.

Toro continued to howl and struggle as I dried him with a towel while fending off the protector. When I finally released him, he took over the grooming in his usual fashion, with Miss Kitty sniffing him carefully to be sure he was all right. Then I worried about what he might be ingesting that hadn't been removed by the rinsing. I kept him under close scrutiny until he was completely dry and started chasing Miss Kitty around again. The impromptu bath didn't appear to cause any harm. Disaster number 872 avoided.

They are a delightful duo but that's not the way the cat sitters describe them when I am away on Christmas visits. They describe them as the Devastating Duo. The sitters got tired of daily picking up the Christmas decorations knocked to the floor, or the cards scattered across the room and just stashed the enticing objects in a closet for the duration.

Very different personalities have developed. Just because Toro wants to go outside in frigid weather doesn't mean Miss Kitty will. When I ask her if she wants to go too, she looks at me from her warm spot by the wood stove as if I must be crazy to even suggest it! During wood stove season I frequently find them up against the stone platform that holds the stove – sometimes basting their backs and at other times toasting their tummies.

A favorite wintertime spot. Photo/Boots

They both circle my legs to be picked up on occasion but that's where the similarity ends. She doesn't want to be held for very long, nor too tightly and is soon struggling toward the floor. He will settle down for a nice long hug and snuggles up to my neck until one of us decides we've had enough. They both offer loud purrs to let me know they enjoy it.

More than once Miss Kitty has sent me into a frantic search for her when I knew she was inside the house but not in any of her usual napping spots – which vary for both cats according to where the sun is shining or what time of day it is. I have learned to open every closed door because she doesn't cry to be released. Sometimes Toro has alerted me by sniffing under doors. She has been trapped in the garage, in the linen closet, in the pantry, in the bedroom closet and even in the closet housing the water heater under the stairs. That usually occurs when I am seasonally resetting the clock on the device that turns the water heater on and off to take advantage of the Watt Watcher program at off-peak times. Once she was in there overnight before she finally did cry out so I could locate her. I don't think she learned anything from it though. I still need to be vigilant before I close doors. When seasons are changing and it gets a little chilly in the house, she knows how to handle it. She crawls up under the bedspread for a warm nap.

Toro has always been choosy about what canned cat food he will eat, while Miss Kitty will eat anything. She is Miss Piggy and he is Mr. Snacker. He wants to eat a little, then leave it and come back to it later, but if he does that, she moves in to finish his food, resulting in one fat cat. After Miss Kitty developed an intolerance to Vitamin A or E, I had to delete fish from her diet – and consequently from Toro's. At present they are both on diets for senior cats and getting only hard food unless I slip them something from my plate. Now trips to Dr. Brown include a bag of less-fat senior food. I don't understand why they don't slim down in the summer because they spend a great deal of their time prowling the woods and running up and down the hillside. In the winter, as senior cats twelve years old at this writing, they sleep a lot so I chase them up and down the stairs sometimes for exercise.

Miss Kitty, now rivaling Garfield, the original Fat Cat, likes to sleep on the top of the back of the swivel chair as I read or watch TV, while Toro is most likely asleep on my lap. As I say, they live here too, so after I get into bed, they join me, on top of the covers. Toro jumps up gently and stations himself near my upper torso, but not touching me. Miss Kitty plops down with a thud, nestled against me either behind the bend in my legs or in the front of my curved back. Getting out of bed in the middle of the night requires the agility of a contortionist as I inch my way to the headboard, swivel my body while pulling up my legs and then gingerly bringing my feet to the floor. Meanwhile, the cats slumber on, not helping me in the least.

Because of the altitude, my age and family heart history, my doctor recently determined that I needed to use a small amount of oxygen at night. A machine was introduced to the bedroom to provide that. It is a condenser that converts room air to almost pure oxygen and distributes it to my nose through a tube. When the technician who was setting it up for me turned on the machine, it emitted a series of three beeps similar to the ones on excavating machines when operating in reverse. At the first "beep," both cats bolted from the vicinity of the bedroom to places of safety. It was almost a week before they ventured into the bedroom while the machine was running. They gradually accepted it and came back to sleep on the bed again, showing no reaction now when the beeps begin.

The hiding spot of choice for Toro is scrunched up behind the washer/dryer. Under the bed is second choice. For Miss Kitty it is either under the bed or under the bedside circular table with its floor length covering. If their escape to those spots is cut off, they dash down the stairs to the lower level behind one of the two couches.

Shortly after the cats came to live with me, they had their first encounter with a raccoon, through the screen door. Miss Kitty arched her back, fur fluffed out and menaced her way sideways to scare the animal more than twice her size. Chicken Toro ran away from the door, safely back by the refrigerator and watched the adventure Miss

Kitty was having. The adult raccoon wasn't intimidated by the posturing or the hissing and continued to watch her with interest. Miss Kitty didn't venture all the way up to the door, and probably didn't really know what to do next. The raccoon ended the incident by walking away. *Then* Toro came forth to look over the situation, and to see if he could take credit for the rout.

The April following the beginning of their residency with me brought five nightmarish days. One Saturday evening I was entertaining three couples from the neighborhood. Two of the men were quite hard of hearing and the third had problems, too. That meant all of us were talking and laughing louder than usual and that alarmed the cats. One of the guests went out to his car to get something and left the door open. Toro saw his chance and raced out of the house. As I came to close the door – too late – I glimpsed him speeding up the circular drive, crossing the road and on up the hill on the other side, traveling like greased lightning. I called and called him, to no avail. After the guests left, I went up and down the road, again calling out his name. Then I reasoned that after everything was quiet and he was sure they were all gone, he would come home. I "left a light on" for him and checked the deck periodically during the night. Meanwhile, Miss Kitty was keeping a vigil for him, too. With the coming of daylight there was still no Toro.

I posted a note on the community bulletin board, informed the vet of his departure, notified the pet program on the radio and put an ad in the newspaper of a lost cat. I heard nothing from any of those activities and kept up my search of the neighborhood, calling and calling him by name. I can just imagine that the neighbors listening to me were feeling sorry for me – "that poor woman!" Miss Kitty was upset too, an attitude caught from me, no doubt, so in order not to upset her further, I would get into the shower to do my crying.

When I turned into Forest Lakes as I came from choir practice the following Wednesday night, I thought, *maybe he will be on the deck waiting to be let in!* I had thought that every time I came up the hill and told myself to be reasonable, that he wouldn't be there and was lost and gone forever. I continued driving and crying (not easy) and drove into the garage. As I came around the back of the car, I thought I heard a faint *meow*. And there he was! He looked a little thinner but not as thin as I had expected. Chipmunks and birds were available and snowmelt was running in the streams giving him access to water, so he could take care of himself.

I eagerly opened the door to the house for him, calling to Miss Kitty that Toro was back! She came running and gave him the sniffing inspection of his life, even while he was eating. The prodigal son had returned.

It was a day or two before I had the courage to let him out again, but in the meantime he had stuck pretty close to me in the house. When I finally did let them both out, I went out frequently to see what they were doing and if I didn't see them, I called out, "I don't see my babies! I don't see Toro! I don't see Miss Kitty!" and they would come running! That was a relief to me. *They* wanted to stay close to home, too.

There have been no more repeats of that adventure by either of them, although they have each had their turns at staying out later than I want them to. This activity results in either leaving on the deck light or the lamp near the deck door so I can spend a good part of the night peeking out my bedroom door to see if the wanderer is on the deck. It makes me nervous because I am never sure just what is rambling around out there in the dark woods that might regard a cat as a nice midnight snack.

When I am working at the computer and one of them wants me to do something specific, they either meow by the chair (Miss Kitty), or scratch at the upholstery (Toro) until I get up. As we all march across the room, I know what is wanted by which way they turn. If it is to the right, it is to go outside. If it's the left, the food dishes are empty. I react accordingly.

The cats have been a real joy, entertainment and comfort to me. They are members of my family. Each still comes over to me to be picked up, kissed, and cuddled a little so we both know we are loved. God does provide.

SIXTEEN
Community Involvement

I'm not really a joiner but have been active in church work since sixth grade when an older sister shanghaied me into singing tenor in her junior choir. Sometimes I have been a little resentful of my mother's advice: *If you have a talent, you should use it when called upon.* Now, at this late stage, I am learning how to say NO, nicely, of course. In August of 1984, having arrived in Forest Lakes in mid-July, I sought out the Bayfield Presbyterian Church of the Pine River and before too many months passed, I was involved in the choir, again singing tenor but this time as the result of a bad throat infection picked up in Florida which sent my vocal range plummeting. I'm glad it didn't go on to make me a bass! Soon I became a member of the adult potluck group, the Crusaders Club, serving a stint as Vice President in charge of obtaining programs.

Then I was an Elder for six years and during that time suggested the establishment of a church newsletter. We called it *The Presby Press*, a name suggested by a Mormon friend. Guess who did that for five years?

As is usual in a small church, members need to wear many hats to get all the work accomplished. I served on several committees, including a long-term commitment on the building committee charged with renovating the fellowship hall, adding a new kitchen and two new restrooms. The former restroom area was revamped and the space added to the sanctuary. Later, as a member of the church Centennial Committee I organized and wrote the second 50-year history for the year-long Centennial Celebration.

Maybe I am a slow learner. I should have known by this time in my life that if you suggest a new program, you are commissioned to implement it. For a number of years I had been complaining that most churches, including ours, were falling down on the job of helping parents, especially young ones, in the art of Christian parenting. In the fall of 1999, I found myself volunteering to lead such a class when no one else spoke up. When I returned home from that meeting, one of my little voices exploded, declaring that I surely must be crazy to volunteer for that at age 77. But I know what force was behind the action, as He has pushed me several times before.

So far, I am in my fifth year at it and the bonus is that I am enjoying it. Calling on my years of experience in leading youth groups and as a parent of two children, I am literally writing the curriculum each week. My goal is that each week, class members will take home at least one Christian parenting tip they can put into action immediately. The classroom has two large tables pushed together, with chairs placed around the perimeter. This enables everyone to have eye contact with each other. My husband and I used this room arrangement when we taught the high school Sunday school class back in Illinois. It eliminated any "back row" whispering or inattention by the young people. Parents can interrupt at any time, giving all of us the benefit of their experiences that do or do not work in this important task of child rearing. The class is frequently events-driven when something of major proportions takes place in the community or the nation. We take up that event and save the prepared class notes for another time.

The class notes, and other helpful material gleaned from wherever, are printed and distributed in each class. Members who miss classes are encouraged to pick up the missed material the next time they are present. I keep asking, "You *are* filing these away in a folder, aren't you?" I am hoping parents will refer to them when these situations come up with subsequent children, or when a previously discussed subject becomes relevant. (Hmmm, maybe another book?)

Shortly after I arrived in Forest Lakes, I joined the Bayfield Study Club, meeting once a month in the homes of the members. This club founded the Bayfield Public Library in the early '30s, amidst the Great Depression, through a variety of fund-raising events, and still supports it as well as other worthy causes to benefit the community. I took my turn as Secretary and at the helm of this organization too.

Less than five months after my arrival, I got politically involved in Forest Lakes through election to the Board of the Property Owners Association for six years. Then I took on the Covenants Committee (you know how much fun that is – telling people they must follow the rules), helping to rewrite the covenants and seeing it through to adoption. I was elected twice to serve on the Board of the Forest Lakes Metropolitan District (provides road maintenance, water, sewer, some recreation), serving for eight years. I declined to run again, being a firm believer in term limits. I was off for about two months and was asked to accept an appointment to fill a resignation vacancy on the board, for about 18 months. Term limits? Sigh. I still believe that term limits in Congress would go a long way to eliminate the excessive power of long-time members. It's supposed to be a citizen legislature for brief periods of service, not career positions.

One summer day in 1988, Monte Wommer, then Chief of our Upper Pine River Fire District, made a surprise visit to my door. We stood out on the ramp while he made his unusual request. A training session for volunteer fire fighters and EMTs was scheduled to be held soon and he wanted me to fake a heart attack as part of the exercise. Monte and I were fellow choir members and joked around a lot. Maybe he thought I was a "character" and therefore, a character actress.

My first reaction was that I didn't think I could do it but after he supplied more details, I thought maybe I could pull it off. The day came, but doing yard work in the bright sunshine gave my face a nice rosy glow. That wouldn't make me look like a heart attack victim! Before the performance I tried out several shades of face powder to reduce the glow. No good. Inspiration led me to the flour canister. Ah! That worked! But I have to tell you – flour is not as soft as face powder. It was grainy, but I could stand it for a short time.

Following Monte's instructions, I brought along a bag of trash to leave in the dumpster located near the fire station. He told me ahead of time that the training was about to start and that the area would be temporarily closed to residents during that time but that I should try to convince whoever would stop me that I just wanted to dump that bag and would leave immediately. I wasn't having much luck with the volunteer who didn't want me there but Monte strolled over and said to let me do it and then they'd start the training. She didn't like it but let me continue.

I parked near the dumpster, grabbed my trash bag and tossed it in, gasping in pain while letting my warm hands slide down the metal container to cool them as much as possible. Down on the ground, I clutched my chest, moaning that it hurt. They were all watching me and some rushed over with a stretcher. I started to get up but they stopped me, saying they would put me on the stretcher. They checked vital signs while asking me questions: Has this happened before? No. How old are you? 66. Is there family heart history? Yes, both parents died of heart attacks at 66 and 68, a brother at age 43 of diabetes and heart complications, as well as several uncles. I answered every question truthfully, except for claiming the pain. Even if the vital signs were O.K., the family history probably convinced them to take no chances.

While this was going on, another volunteer went to the phone to summon an ambulance from Mercy Medical Center. At that point, Monte stopped them, explaining that it was part of the training session. He added, to me, that if an ambulance had come, it would have cost me $200. Still in my acting mode, I replied that it would have cost *him* $200.

I assured the volunteers that if it really had been an attack, I would want them to be on hand because they acted so quickly and efficiently.

Monte told me several days later that some of the volunteers resented it – they thought they had been tricked – but he told them their response might have been different had they known it wasn't real. I guess I really *did* give an Academy Award performance!

My real-life experience with the emergency room came 15 years later when the third try at high blood pressure medication also caused rashes to break out on various parts of my body. I discontinued the pills, informed my doctor of that "rash decision" and received a prescription for the fourth attempt at control. I would wait for the extreme itching to subside before taking it. Yes, indeed, advancing age has forced me to join the "pill poppers" but I don't let it take over my life. If I can improve a situation by changes in diet or activity, I do it. If not, I accept what advantages medical technology can offer me and resume my normal activities.

While in between blood pressure medications, I was baking a cake to take to a Crusaders Club potluck one day. I checked on its progress and when I stood up after looking in the oven, I felt a little dizzy and lightheaded. I sat on the couch while the cake finished baking. When the buzzer went off and I removed the cake from the oven, I experienced the same slight dizziness. Back to the couch to lie down. When the lightheadedness didn't go away entirely, I thought it wiser not to get into the car to go down the hill for my mail. I called niece Anne to see if she would get it for me, explaining the request. She immediately said she would call neighbor Dick Vaccaro who was also a First Responder for the volunteer fire department to check on me. I didn't think that was necessary but said *I* would call him. I did and he came, used his blood pressure machine and got a high reading, took my pulse and then contacted his crew to come. Dick and his wife Dottie were aware of my high blood pressure and that I used oxygen at night. I knew Dick was thinking of a possible stroke when he hooked me up to oxygen. That produced a little lower reading but when three crew members arrived, they did an EKG, again took blood pressure and pulse, drew some blood, checked for blood sugar level and consulted with each other. Meanwhile, I am telling them it is much ado about nothing and that except for the slight dizziness, I felt fine.

The rescue crews had seen episodes like this due to our high altitude and, coupled with the period of taking no blood pressure reducing pills for almost a month and with my family heart history, recommended that I go to the ER to be checked by a doctor even though the EKG showed no heart problem.

I reluctantly agreed, insisting that I could walk up the ramp to their vehicle, trailing the oxygen tubing behind. They strapped me to a gurney and took me down the hill to a better-equipped ambulance for the ride to Durango. At Mercy Medical Center, the ER personnel checked everything over again, adding a urinalysis that indicated a low-grade urinary tract infection. That really surprised me because I had experienced none of the symptoms you would expect of that malady. The doctor prescribed sulfa and gave me enough pills to get me started on the series.

By this time it was about 8:30 p.m. and because I had not eaten dinner, a meal was ordered for me. It was a box lunch, similar to what you get on some airlines. The box contained a turkey sandwich on wheat bread, a packet of mayo, a bag of potato chips, a small container of applesauce with two graham crackers and a packaged brownie. As I ate, I read the nutritional information on the chips and the brownie...it added up to a virtual heart attack in bags! What irony – I was there primarily because of high blood pressure and slight dizziness. I ate only a few chips and none of the brownie but the sandwich plus a little of the mayo, applesauce and crackers tasted good and satisfied me. I gladly called my niece Anne for transportation when they told me I could go home and we arrived there about 10:45 p.m.

I took the first sulfa pill that night and again after the recommended 12 hour intervals over the next 5 days. How come I kept feeling worse? My appetite was terrible, I didn't sleep well and the slight dizziness was still there. Over the weekend, my nurse daughter-in-law said I should see my doctor on Monday. When I called his office, he was on vacation but I talked to his nurse who was aware of my medical history. After she consulted with the doctor on call, he agreed to see me the next morning. That night was the mother-of-all-bad-nights, spending much of it in the bathroom with retching bile attacks. When the doctor heard my story, he said I should stop the sulfa pills, start on the new BP medication, and stay on the cholesterol-lowering drug. Apparently I was allergic to sulfa which I could not recall having taken before. The ER doctor had quizzed me about allergies to medication and I reported those I was aware of so he cannot be faulted for my miseries. I was amazed at how quickly I began to feel better after stopping the sulfa. Life began to be worth living again.

About this second contact with EMTs I again have to say that the treatment was prompt and efficient and I applaud their dedication to duty. We are fortunate to have these Good Samaritans in our communities and in our emergency rooms. Here is a salute and my thanks to Dick, Mike, Matt, Jan, Shane, Lisa, Dr. DeBonde, Laura, Dr. Jeff and my niece Anne for all their assistance.

I don't know of many families that don't have traumatic events overtake them on occasion. While I was deeply engulfed in church, civic and community commitments during the mid-nineties, our entire family was coming to grips with agony and anxieties as Rick and Joann wrestled with unfortunate incidents following the untimely death at age 26 of their son Tony Perkins of congenital heart problems. He left behind two boys, Andrew, four, and Joey, one, and an ex-wife who was not cut out for motherhood, and that comment is being very kind to her. I won't go into the details of the horrible lives those boys endured under her "care." It would read like a soap opera. But one night Rick and Joann called me in utter frustration at what was happening, seeking advice. They said they thought they had three options: A: Just walk away from the entire situation and have nothing to do with the two boys and their mother. B: Do what they could to work with the system in Florida to rehabilitate the mother. Experience had taught them that this would be extremely difficult and chaotic to their lives in what seemed like insurmountable odds. Even then they could not control what the mother did. Or C: If Option

B didn't work, eventually petition to adopt the boys, thereby terminating the mother's parental rights.

I thought about their options for a few minutes and then said that, knowing both of them and of their love and concern for the boys, I didn't think they could possibly go with Option A. Under Option B their mother would undermine what little they could do through visitation with the boys. If they were willing to do it, I thought Option C would be their best chance at rescuing the boys from bleak and uncertain futures.

Considering the speed of their agreement with my assessment, I think they had already come to that conclusion but needed the confirmation. What followed was five more years of frustration for all of us after Rick and Joann were granted temporary custody of the boys by a Florida court. This came about because the mother continued to neglect her sons and failed to comply with court-ordered changes in her life. Rick and Joann documented everything regarding her phone calls and visitation. The mother did not appear in court, nor was she represented at either of the two adoption hearings.

On March 19, when the various agencies, psychologists, school officials and other witnesses completed their reports and the judge declared that Andrew and Joey could be adopted by Rick and Joann, there was not a dry eye in the courtroom. The judge asked if he could inform the boys. To protect them from hearing details of the reports, Andrew and Joey had been waiting across the street at the library. When the boys came in and were given the news, a pale-faced Drew asked the judge if anyone could take this apart. The judge assured him that they couldn't, but the other side of it was that now the boys were stuck with Rick and Joann as their parents! This is a good time to mention that on their church calendar, March 19 celebrates the Feast of St. Joseph. St. Joseph has been looking after all of us. Tony could rest well in heaven.

A year later on March 19, at a celebration dinner, Rick asked the boys if being adopted was anything like they expected. Almost in unison they shouted, "Better!" News of that response brought tears

114

to the eyes of all of us.

It has been a pleasure to watch the boys lose their many fears and develop their talents while settling in to be a real family. I would strongly urge anyone close to or with knowledge of a child abuse or neglect situation to consider adoption. It might be a rescue mission. In too many cases, the natural mother is NOT the best person to raise the children. I am so proud of Rick and Joann for taking on that great responsibility as they approach middle age.

The new family two years after adoption. Photo/Rick Brenner

Somewhere along the line in my community involvement I was summoned for jury duty and selected to serve on a three-member jury. Is that exclusive to Colorado? I had never heard of that before. My jury partners were reasonable people and we correctly found the defendant guilty of a business contest scam, which he had to make right with the winner.

I was active in Mercy Medical Center Auxiliary for about eight years, going to Durango to operate the beverage cart each Tuesday morning when weather, illness or vacation didn't prevent me. Wanting to devote more time to getting *Guidelines and Guardrails* published, I bowed out of that responsibility

And just what is *Guidelines and Guardrails?* My late husband and I had led the Youth Fellowship group at our Presbyterian church in Kankakee, Illinois, for 12 consecutive years. We took a few years off from that responsibility but when our daughter entered high school, the teacher for that age group retired and no one else came forward to teach it, so we stepped into the gap. (My mother's voice again?) We did that for six more years, until our son graduated from high school, when we wanted more freedom to visit the kids at college on a weekend now and then.

Fast forward to my house in the woods. I had always intended to write a book about our experiences for high school youth leaders who are willing to volunteer but have little experience. I had brought along a lot of the material we used but had done nothing about it, what with setting up a new household. The time came when I was aware of gentle prodding from God to get with it. After pushing the nudgings to the back of my mind for several years, I could finally ignore them no longer.

My kids suggested I get a computer, which would make the job easier and faster. My son recommended one for me and I was off and running. I had a little computer experience before retiring so it wasn't too hard to make it do what I wanted – most of the time. A dear knowledgeable friend from the church, Elizabeth Testa, agreed to edit the book for me so I funneled the chapters to her as they rolled off the computer printer. In the meantime, I submitted query letters and sample chapters to publishers while continuing to write the book. I had racked up about 30 or so rejection slips (some nice and personal – others form letters) when I decided I needed to drop some of my activities and concentrate on the book. By the time it was completed, there were 25 chapters, and 42 rejections. Now there are 43 rejections, and that last one hurts.

One morning in November of 1998, the phone rang and when I answered it I was a little testy because I had just been plagued by unwanted marketing calls. When the caller asked to speak to "Beulah" and had difficulty pronouncing my legal name, I figured it was another marketing call, so I answered by asking, "What are you selling?"

Surprised, she said, "I'm not selling anything! I want to talk to her about her manuscript."

Then I was embarrassed, and apologizing profusely, explained why I had answered that way. When our conversation ended, I was floating somewhere up near the ceiling. The publisher wanted me to send the entire manuscript! Of course, I sent it off the next day. They later determined they liked it and wanted to do a feasibility study. They contacted their booksellers, described the book and asked them to estimate how many copies they thought they could sell. The publisher's bottom line necessary to make a profit was 20,000 copies and my book came up 2,000 copies short. I came down from the ceiling where I had been all this time. It was some time before I could summon the spirit to contact other publishers.

I understand that it is very expensive to publish a book – and most publishers are reluctant to take a chance on unknown writers but I am pushing on. I still feel God prodded me to write it, and also that therefore there is a publisher out there for it somewhere.

SEVENTEEN
Social Life

Since the Koskis had already introduced me to a number of people who would be my neighbors before I moved to Colorado, it was easy to continue with dinners in each other's homes and at potlucks with larger groups. My friends soon learned that I was not a drinker. If they wanted to drink, that was their decision, but I was not going to buy alcohol for anyone, so when they came to my house for meals it was on a Bring Your Own Bottle arrangement or someone volunteered to provide the bar. I appreciated the fact that they always had soft drinks or juices at their houses for me. It worked fine for both of us.

One of my new friends, Peg Dexter, and I had many agreeable political discussions, complaining about what we might see on television, or during political campaigns. "Now if *we* were in charge …!" We were like-minded.

I also had social interaction with people at the church and it was some of them who re-introduced dancing into my life. When I was in high school I loved to dance and in my immaturity I thought if a boy didn't dance, he wasn't worth looking at twice. We had Noon Dances in the gym during lunch hour where a non-dancer manned the record player. Not a boom box, not a stereo nor a disc player – just a plain old-fashioned record player. One particular partner and I were really into ballroom dancing and we spent a lot of time practicing. (I wonder where he is now?) Another fellow a year younger than I would dance only with me when "Josephine" was played, so that was a given but I never knew why.

Several years after graduation, I married a man who didn't dance at all! Gil did this out of deference to his parents who thought dancing was a sure pathway to sin. (Remember, this was in the forties.) To my surprise, I didn't miss the dancing at all – so at least I had my priorities right by that time and recognized that qualities of kindness, reverence and a great sense of humor were more important than the ability to dance.

In Colorado, two couples from the church, Ruth and Dick Berry and Ed and Evelyn Wommer, took me dancing at the Senior Center in Durango. I enjoyed it very much and found that I hadn't lost the touch although I was a little rusty at first. Some of the wives had to limit their participation because of physical difficulties so they didn't mind if their husbands twirled the singles around now and then. One of the fellows in particular always sought me out for the "Beer Barrel Polka," which left both of us happy but breathless. Other wives seemed not too pleased by it, maybe regarding me as a threat – the Merry Widow – but all I wanted to do with their husbands was dance – not seduce them!

Romance? One widower I met at the dances volunteered to cut down some of my pine trees that had been recommended for removal by the Forest Service. He came several times and was very proficient at the task. I helped where I could, and provided him with lunch. He wanted to take the relationship further but I wasn't interested in him in that way. Only later did I learn, though he didn't look it, that he was 17 years older than I, and I was no spring chicken even then.

Another one, a retired auto mechanic, plied me with car lubricants and also wanted me to give him more time than just at the dances. I told him there just weren't any sparks for me, and that was essential. He didn't want to take "no" for an answer and begged me to go out with him more – that maybe the sparks would come after all.

I reluctantly agreed but after two weeks or so, I called a halt to it.

A third one, also one of the dancers, began pressing his case, with some positive reaction from me, but I think there were two things influencing the end of that. When he brought me home one night and I unlocked the door, we were assailed by a terrible odor from the litter box for my new kittens that had been de-wormed by the vet the day before. I later learned he was feuding with a neighbor about the odor emanating from her property. She had *lots* and *lots* of cats in and around her house!

The other influence was that he got lost leaving Forest Lakes that night and spent a couple of hours driving around, trying to find the exit. We have a number of dead end roads but he should have realized that he needed to keep going down hill to get off the mountain. No doubt he was convinced that I represented nothing but trouble.

Since I didn't have a regular partner, the dances ceased to be that enjoyable so I found other things to occupy my twice-monthly Saturday nights. A fellow at church had lost his wife recently and we exchanged dinner invitations a couple of times. That began to look somewhat promising. I left to visit children at Christmas and it was agreed that I would call somewhere along the line to let him know what time he could pick me up at the airport on my return. There was no answer when I tried calling for a couple of days and since my departure time was near, I made other arrangements to be picked up.

He finally called sometime after I returned home and said he had been on a little trip with another widow but declared that it didn't mean anything. He said he wanted to see me. I invited him to attend a *Music in the Mountains Concert* to be held at the beautiful Tamarron Resort north of Durango on a coming Sunday afternoon, along with a neighbor couple, Peggy and Roger Minner. We agreed on a time he would come to my house where the Minners would pick us up. When he didn't arrive at the appointed time I called him. He had taken a nap and overslept and would be there in a jiffy. He didn't live too far away so our timing was still on schedule. Soon he came roaring down my driveway and slewed to a stop. I realized he had imbibed a little too much. I was glad he wouldn't be driving us to the concert. Peggy and Roger picked us up and soon he was pawing me in the back seat! He had always been such a gentleman, and had never even kissed me.

While he was in the restroom at the resort, I told my friends that I had no experience with drunks and didn't know what to do. They told me to try to ignore his behavior at the concert, which involved talking out loud and frequent trips to the restroom. Peggy said that we would go get something to eat afterwards, which might help the situation. It did, but not much. The plan was to come back to my house for dessert, which we did, but Peggy and Roger made sure he left before they did. And that was the end of that. I considered it a narrow escape. Sometime later I learned that he had married again, and (did you guess?) it was the widow he had taken on a trip.

As I had been saying for some time, "No husband is better than the wrong one!" And besides, after making all the decisions of my life for some years – what time to eat, where to go, when to go to bed and when to arise, how to spend my money – by now I was too independent and probably no man would be able to live with me. Also, with a husband around, would I be able to continue to write? I decided then to really get serious about finishing my book. So much for romance. I would continue to be open on the subject but would not go searching for it. What will be will be.

One year I planned to drive back to my hometown of Oconomowoc, Wisconsin, for the 60th High School Reunion. When the time came, however, my car was in need of a major repair so I had to cancel. The Reunion Committee later sent me a report of the event. I chuckled as I read it and thought, *you can tell it was for senior citizens because the main banquet was held at noon!* Yes, aging happens to us, but we have a good time in the daylight, too.

EIGHTEEN
Paradise in the Pines

No matter the season, it is beautiful in my piney paradise! And tourists are well aware of this because they come year round – for the scenery, for skiing, biking, hiking, boating, river rafting, camping, horseback riding and just to enjoy the flavor of the Old West. According to the Chamber of Commerce bulletins regarding the area, the sun shines 360 days a year. Maybe it *is* true because if we get two cloudy days in a row, we feel put upon! When I return to Illinois and experience day after day of gray December and January skies, I realize just how precious our sunshine is in the Rocky Mountains.

We all enjoy Christmas cards with snowy mountains, white frosted pine trees providing background for cheerful chickadees or vivid cardinals. Well, when it snows, I enjoy that by just looking out the window. Electric blue Steller's jays, with added splendor of unbelievably blue skies, replace the cardinals on my Christmas card scenes.

Even on days when it snows, the sun manages to shine at least part of the time. And if it is a light snow, it soon disappears. When it snows too heavily for the sun to melt it from my long drive down to the garage, or for me to make a path from the ramp up to the street, I call the professionals. Along about March when I grow weary with even the small amount of shoveling I do, I inform God that since He put the snow there, I'd appreciate it if He would remove it. And He does – with the sunshine.

Spring is usually late in making an appearance in the Rocky Mountains and is often accompanied by snowmelt rushing down the streams and ditches along the roads. Spring rains bring the dirt on our gravel roads to the top, transferring to cars and foolhardy foot travelers. We are glad when the sun shines with vigor to dry it up and the wind finishes the job. The wind in these tall pines produces a variety of sounds – sometimes gently sighing, sometimes like a car coming down the road, and like a freight train when the wind is really strong. Watching entire tree trunks sway takes your breath away.

Summer temperatures can get up in the 90s but unless we are in a severe drought pattern, that doesn't cause too much distress because of our low humidity – often in the teens or lower. The fall season is gorgeous with its muted reds and yellows mingling with the evergreens – like Oriental carpets laid out on the hillsides.

Sometimes when I glance out the window, my head jerks around for a second look. *Is that a mountain lion out there?* Further inspection shows it to be shifting shadows and sunlight on a tan rock. The terrain takes on different appearances as the sun moves around the sky. A rock can look like a visiting rabbit, or even a bear when dusk changes the shadows in the woods. It truly is awesome. (I know the sun doesn't move around in the sky; it's the earth that revolves, but I plead poetic license because that's the way it *appears* to us!)

For the first ten years or so, various men with snowplows on trucks did the snow removal job, but that also tended to remove gravel from the drive and push it over to the side or over the hill. Then I got out there with my little red wagon and shovel and redistributed the gravel again…and again…and again.

There came a day when I needed to find a new snow remover so I checked out the community bulletin board at the mail stop, found a phone number for a snow shoveler and called him. He really *was* a snow *shoveler* – by hand! I thought he would bow out when I told him about my long drive but he thought he could handle it. When he reported for duty, I was a tad dismayed. He had long, unwashed-looking hair, wore earrings and his jacket was in need of contact with a washing machine. His price was right, though, so I decided to give him a try if he was willing to tackle it. He did an excellent job, and in nothing flat. Since it was a cold day, I invited him in for hot chocolate (maybe he would have preferred a different "hot" drink?) while I wrote out the check. He charged by the hour, and because of his speed, this was to my advantage. We had a good philosophical discussion after I confessed to him that I was a bit dubious about hiring him when I first saw him. He said, "I know...my mother doesn't like my long hair and earrings either!" Whenever each of us had time, we got into interesting discussions about anything and everything. We agreed on a number of them...which bears out the adage, "Don't judge a book by its cover."

I discovered he came from a Mormon family, his brother was a sports physician and, if I recall correctly, his sister was studying law. He considered himself to be the black sheep of the family and appeared to be comfortable with that position.

We worked out an agreement that when the district snowplow went by his house, he would take care of my snow removal as soon as he could. He worked by day in construction as a mason, so frequently the snow prevented him from going to that job. He also carried in wood for me when the weather prevented me from taking care of that task.

Alas, his black sheep status intervened and he left the area. He had told me at the end of one winter season that he was thinking about going back to Utah. He had been living with a woman and her children so I guess it was just too easy to "move on." A pity. Back to the snowplow routine.

Paradise in the pines isn't without its perils, though. Most of my neighbors aren't too close (although a new house has just gone up almost across from me), so when I hear strange sounds in the dark of night, I am on my own to deal with it. One night I was awakened by a need to visit the bathroom across the hall. I got out of bed on the side by the windows because I was pinned in by two heavy cats on the other side. *What's that bright light out there?* I asked myself. Then I realized the light was coming from the open garage door, which shouldn't have been open! I couldn't see any shadows cast by anyone or anything in the garage and as I peered into the night, the garage door came down. I took care of my interrupted mission and returned to the windows just in time to see the garage door open again – and immediately close. This happened several times but I wasn't unduly alarmed because the cats were still deep in sleep on the bed. Had there been anyone down there, they would have sought their personal safety zones.

There has to be an explanation for this, I reasoned and put my brain to work. I recalled that the remote control for the door hadn't worked too well that night when I returned from choir practice. *Probably because the push button area on the control is cracked,* was my next thought. But what vibration set it off? It was about 3 a.m. and since I live on a dead end street, there isn't exactly much traffic at that hour. I decided it was an electrical glitch. During this mental conversation with myself, the door had been going up and down. When it came down again, I ran to the electrical box in the laundry room and turned off the switch to the garage. Good! The door was still down. I'll check it out in the morning.

Next morning, I restored electricity to the garage and went down to see what I could do. The vibrations of the automatic closing of the door between the house and garage set it off again, going up and down. More activity when I removed the remote from the visor. Examination of the remote showed that indeed the cracked push button end was too close to the sensor and the slightest movement would set it off – maybe just ordinary house settling. After struggling for a bit to separate the two halves of the remote by brute force I realized that a screwdriver was required. Then I was able to remove the two pieces of the cracked push button, firmly apply duct tape on both sides of the button, being careful to place it so it would not interfere with the metal sensor. With a flourish (and the screwdriver), I secured the two halves together, pushed the button and was rewarded with immediate response from the runaway garage door. After a few more successful test runs with the remote, I declared the problem solved and went upstairs to fix breakfast.

The next peril to paradise in the pines was much more serious, and one I could not fix. In June of 2002, a forest fire was raging north of Durango, on Missionary Ridge. That was 30 miles or so away from me so I wasn't too worried until it continued to grow eastward in my direction. The daily paper kept us well informed of the fire's progress and the evacuations of various developments, with warnings to all of us living in the pines to stay alert.

Our development has an excellent volunteer fire department as part of the Upper Pine Fire Protection District. The Property Owners Association, in cooperation with the volunteer firemen, worked out an evacuation plan and kept us informed of what to do if and when a fire should engulf Forest Lakes. There were evacuation routes for both vehicles and pedestrians, and they maintained a list of residents who might need extra help because of disabilities, illness or age. These people would get special attention to see that they were safe. My niece Anne, who was on the evacuation committee, was incensed that they had me on that list, telling them that I was one old lady who could take care of herself. But I said I was grateful because if we had to walk out, my age could be a problem because of the mountain terrain. I don't scramble up and down the hillsides as I did when I first encountered the mountains. Sometimes I use a metal-pointed walking stick (original purpose to root out weeds). But then again, riding ten miles a day, five days a week, on an exercise bike at a rate of 16 to 20 miles per hour helps keep the knees limber. Appointments and the unexpected sometimes interfere with that commitment, but I get back on schedule as soon as possible.

I might have been able to walk out but what about my two cats? My biggest concern was for their safety. They were reacting to the smoke in the area and the high winds. I finally realized their dislike of strong winds was three-fold: Wind affected their senses of smell, sight and sound. Heavy smoke added to their vision problems. For several days when they had been sitting in front of the door to go outside, and the door was opened, they sat there and sniffed the air thoroughly, their little noses going full speed. Then they retreated from the door. I didn't urge them because I was happy to have them inside if I had to leave quickly. That same sniffing routine was prevalent in bear season. Litter box cleaning was more frequent during those times as they refused to go outside.

We got the word on about June 7th that Forest Lakes was on Pre-evacuation Status, which meant we must be ready to leave at a moment's notice. I had already gathered up a few pictures, business papers and some items of jewelry, extra cat food and water and had placed them in the car, along with the big cage to hold the two cats (34 pounds between them!). I finally packed a few clothes, diskettes containing both manuscripts and other computer files and a few odds and ends selected as I wandered distractedly through the house. I was not very well organized as far as my personal belongings were concerned. When I mentioned to a friend that I had packed a few clothes, I told her I threw in my old underwear. Later she thought about that and told me she had just bought some new underwear and wasn't going to let it burn up! Then I told her I intended to throw the old underwear away instead of washing it. Our minds were in a whirl. Discussions with others later in the year revealed that we all felt as if we were in limbo. *Would we have to leave our homes? Could the firefighters stop the fire?* We continually checked our flying flags to see if they were blowing to the north or to the south. If south, we chewed our nails as the fire was to the north of us. We had difficulty focusing. We would start one task, then leave it before it was finished and go on to another one.

The news of impending danger got worse and the fire was lapping at the backside of our mountain. I knew I had to make hard decisions. The Red Cross had set up an Evacuation Center at Bayfield High School and some residents had already left to go there. My niece Diana and her husband Adolph Hoehn, whose ranch is about 70 miles west of Forest Lakes, near Cortez, had extended an invitation to me and her sister Anne and husband Tony to come there if we had to leave. I quickly accepted because I knew my stranger-wary cats would have a terrible time with crowds of people around at the high school. Anne asked Diana if her new neighbors who had moved to Forest Lakes less than two weeks before could come too since they knew no one in the area. They graciously agreed.

We had not been ordered to evacuate but we were sure that order was coming. Niece Emily and her husband Roger had not yet moved into their house just down the street from me, but that weekend Roger decided to come to the house from Phoenix to check on things. I say God sent him to take care of his wife's ancient aunt.

It was Saturday, June 15th. I invited Roger to eat with me that night and the more we discussed the fire, the more determined we were to leave right away. He went back to his house to rescue a few things while I rounded up the cats and got them, protesting, into the cage on the front seat. Roger returned to put my big suitcase into the car. The portable oxygen tank had to go with me also. We concluded I would follow him because I don't like to drive at night unless I am very familiar with the route. Anne and Tony and their new neighbors decided to wait at least another day.

We left about 9:15 p.m. It was a terrible feeling to shut that door and wonder if my house would still be there for me to return to. In spite of little time, my mind flashed to many memorable scenes of life in my house in the woods. What would the birds and wild animals that had entertained me in exchange for a little food and water do if the fire continued to grow? I had no answer. Feet dragging, I went to the car.

When we got down to the entrance, officers who were checking every car stopped our vehicles. Were we residents? Where did we live? Where are you going? They asked us to check in with the Red Cross at the high school to get on their list of people who had left the area but by then other officials at the high school wouldn't let us turn in there because the lot was full. On to Cortez! I was very grateful that I had Roger's red truck lights to follow. I would call the Red Cross from Cortez the next day to check in.

I was having trouble keeping up with Roger, and when some cars got between us, he pulled over to the side. I followed suit and discovered I was still in second gear...the way I drove in the slow exodus line leaving Forest Lakes! That corrected, I was able to keep up with him.

We got to the ranch about 11:30 p.m., finally getting to bed after midnight. The cats and I were installed in the upstairs bedroom, where the cats would stay in isolation the entire week. Roger went on to Phoenix the next morning and I went to church with Diana and Adolph. Our prayers were fervent.

On Sunday night Anne, Tony, Jan and Orville Lips (the new neighbors) arrived at 10:30. Their entourage included Dutch, a tall miniature Schnauzer belonging to Anne and Tony, and two large black labs, Mac and Maggie, whose owners were Jan and Orville (or "Orv," as we soon called him). Although the cats were safe behind a closed door to the upstairs, as soon as they heard the deep, deep barks of the labs or Dutch's more shrill offerings, they ran to get under something. I can only guess at the trauma they were suffering, after their quiet lives with a quiet old lady. Their stress was evident in the handfuls of fur that came out with each brushing, and the small amounts of food and water they consumed the first few days.

We couldn't have had a more beautiful refugee camp. The Hoehn ranch lies in the shadow of the Sleeping Ute Mountain in southwest Colorado, with rocky outcroppings harboring native Pinon and other trees. A narrow irrigation ditch ran across the yard, providing a wonderful bathtub for the labs and Dutch. It was a great place to cool a watermelon, too.

What was happening back in La Plata County with the Missionary Ridge fire was never very far from our minds. We kept up with details through the *Durango Herald*'s great website, noting that the fire was getting closer and closer to Forest Lakes. The Schriers and the Lips made a few trips back to Durango and Bayfield to take care of some previous appointments, pick up the mail and papers, any new information and some items from my house, belatedly considered. Although I hadn't mentioned it, Anne knew the wood carving of a bear (like my spiritual bear) given to me by Barb was special to me, so she put it in the refrigerator to protect it from fire. That impressed me, I wouldn't have thought of that. She also stashed my precious guest book there. My children and friends kept up with events through the newspaper's website, phone calls and e-mails.

"Meanwhile back at the ranch," our gracious hosts tried to carry on with business as usual. Diana fulfilled her commitment to the Cortez Hospital as a volunteer and Adolph took his scheduled three-day post as a firewatcher high up in a tower in the forest. Tony and Orv did repair work on a porch railing, helped with the irrigating and even went over to visit Adolph in his lonely tower. The women took turns with the laundry, cooking and shopping whenever we could persuade Diana to turn some jobs over to us.

Diana had a pattern for special neck coolers made for her local volunteer firefighters so we obtained material and Anne, Jan and I set up an assembly line to make as many of them as possible for all the fire departments. Jan cut out the patterns, Anne sewed them part way and I filled the cavities with polymer crystals. Anne completed the sewing. The crystals absorb moisture from sweating necks and in the process keep the firemen cool. I don't know how many we made but Jan and Anne continued to make them when we returned to Forest Lakes, with minimum assistance from me.

In between those tasks, we had some wild domino games. We were a genial, jovial bunch in spite of the shadow of disaster hanging over us. Orv cracked us all up one day with his recital of events of the night before when he left his bedroom during the night for a trip to the bathroom. At the same time, I was returning from my trip to the bathroom. There was a small nightlight somewhere in the area that cast anyone in its orbit in partial shadow. Orv is tall and (dare I say it?) a little portly. In my "prime" I was 5'1" but now can only stretch the measuring rod up to about 4'8". As I rounded the corner into the kitchen, Orv approached the same spot, calling forth a surprised "Oh!" from each of us. I graciously yielded my space on the bathroom trail and returned to my bedroom. As he told it the next day, "I was startled to see this midget who was below my radar in the middle of the night." As if the midnight midget could have intimidated "Big Orv"!

On Saturday morning June 22nd, we got the word that we could come back to Forest Lakes. We all packed up and took off about 10 a.m., leaving Diana and Adolph to their peace and quiet again. When I got to the Forest Lakes entrance, officers were stopping all cars and checking license plates, to be sure we were residents who belonged there. That was good because we had heard there was burglarizing in some of the evacuated subdivisions, but not ours. Those of a criminal bent are always looking for opportunities. I'm happy to report that the fellows who were committing the crimes were later caught and forced to make restitution to their victims as well as receiving other punishment, including prison time.

I was told to go in the house and first check that everything was O.K., no power outages, etc., and then bring in some things but to stay alert and listen for sirens in case the wind shifted and we had to leave again. We remained on that alert level for several weeks, returning to the distracted behavior we experienced before receiving the evacuation order. We were nervous and restless. This went on until the danger diminished, not only with this fire but also for the whole season.

I walked into my house at 12:30 p.m. After checking it over, I went back to release the cats from their bondage in the cage. They were so glad to be home, they went straight from the car into the house, without checking out the yard or the forest! It took them awhile to give the entire house the sniff tests to be sure everything was O.K. The smoke smell made them nervous and cautious for quite some time afterward.

In spite of the peculiar feeling I had when I turned my key in the lock to leave on the 15th, wondering if the home I had dreamed of, prayed for and worked for would be there when I returned, it was a good experience because I was forced to re-think what is important and what is just "stuff." My cats were safe; my relatives, friends and neighbors were safe.

As recommended by the Forest Service, I have had a number of trees cut down to insure "defensible space," even though there was already quite a bit of clear area around my house. After I got used to those changes, I liked it and decided it made the lot look better. A year later, with continued drought only a little less severe than in 2002, we were again consumed by fire concerns; in fact lightning started a small fire recently on the Bureau of Land Management property next to Forest Lakes. We are always on the alert.

Eventually, the deer came back to Forest Lakes, but because of the continued drought and the lack of munchables, they looked so thin you could see their ribs. The community water pan, a location in my yard well known to birds, deer, skunks, raccoons, bears, dogs and who knows what else, holding two to three gallons, was popular, needing to be filled more than once daily during the drought. Raccoons came back to the deck for their nightly handouts, many times draining the deck water dish. People who live higher up on the mountain told of seeing a bear with singed skin. The wildlife suffer from fires, too.

A few embers from the other side of our mountain had crossed over the ridge but spot firefighters were on them immediately and kept them from spreading. There were no structures in that area. All of us in the Missionary Ridge fire have nothing but praise for the professional firefighters who came here from across the country. They did an excellent job of protecting most of the homes in that huge fire of 70,085 acres, losing only 56 homes and 27 outbuildings. Sadly, one federal firefighter lost his life when a burned-out tree toppled on him on his first day on the job.

The cost of fighting the fire was $40.8 million. In return, residents of La Plata County showed their gratitude and appreciation by volunteering in Red Cross Evacuation Centers, supplying the firefighters with food, clothing and equipment, granting them free passage to entertainment venues and restaurants and anything else they could think of to say thanks. Several months after the fire the local newspapers were still printing letters of thanks to us from the firefighters or their families with the common theme: They have never felt so warmly received in a community across the nation than they were in Durango and Bayfield.

I'm sure you are aware of the battle waging between environmentalists and forest management people who want to thin the forests and get rid of the dead underbrush. The plan to use loggers to do some of this is what has set off the environmentalists. The battle still wages, but from where I sit among the pines, I vote for thinning and clearing and less intense fires in the future!

Philosophically speaking, it's good to take calendar in hand to review the year that is about to pass into oblivion, even if you don't send annual Christmas letters. When you review the year, you experience the busy-ness, the good times, the joys and, yes, even the pains that add up to a year of your life. You read between the date-lines to remember what you didn't record...the pleasurable yard work; walks along the mountain roads or through the woods; stacking the wood pile; watching the curious wildlife; majestic scenery; shoveling snow; the friends who stopped by to bring a book, a sample from their kitchens or just to talk.

And in the year of the fire my annual review saw the week when everything noted had to be rescheduled...and when I prayed gratefully that I was still in my piney paradise.

Whether you live in the city or the country, there will be pleasure and pain in your surroundings and in family life. There are always risks in life and to run from all of them almost translates into having no life. If you have a dream, pursue it. Research the probabilities and possibilities to be sure they are attainable in your circumstances. Then – go for it!

Kicking and screaming – that's the way I will leave if it becomes necessary – like animals in cartoons that brace all four legs on the doorway when someone wants to pull them through. I will not go gently. I hope all the animals and birds would rally around as if to plead, "Don't make her go! She is our lifeline!"

In spite of the pre-moving agony, the things that went wrong during construction, the fizzled romances, the impassioned civic and charitable activities and *because of* the feathered and furred domestic and wild companions, the many good friends, and relatives nearby, I can sum it up in two words: Vast contentment.

Paradise and peril in the pines – I'll take it!